TV LAMPS

to light the WORLD

identification & value guide

John A. Shuman III

COLLECTOR BOOKS
A Division of Schroeder Publishing Co., Inc.

Front cover: Madeira red chess horse head, 10" long, 14" high, $100.00 – 125.00. Ornate ivory sampan trimmed in gold carrying Chinese couple, $70.00 – 90.00. Apple green plaster-of-Paris hearth, two flower/candleholders, airbrushed sandstone and black German shepherd, 14" wide, 9" high, $135.00 – 150.00.

Back cover: Purple and cream/brown young double ducklings on blue-green porcelain driftwood, 12" wide, 9" high, $125.00 – 150.00. Molded cast iron galleon with cutouts, gilded with black and green staining, bright red clip holds chipped glass disk, backlighted, diameter of the disk 8", ship measures 9½" wide and 9" high, $85.00 – 100.00. Apple green/light green and ivory Deco gazelle on a six-scrolled base, 13" wide, 10¼" high, $75.00 – 95.00.

Cover design by Beth Summers
Book design by Heather Warren

COLLECTOR BOOKS
P.O. Box 3009
Paducah, Kentucky 42002-3009

www.collectorbooks.com

Copyright © 2006 by John A. Shuman III

The current values in this book should be used only as a guide. They are not intended to set prices, which vary from one section of the country to another. Auction prices as well as dealer prices vary greatly and are affected by condition as well as demand. Neither the author nor the publisher assumes responsibility for any losses that might be incurred as a result of consulting this guide.

Searching for a Publisher?

We are always looking for people knowledgeable within their fields. If you feel that there is a real need for a book on your collectible subject and have a large comprehensive collection, contact Collector Books.

C
O
N
T
E
N
T
S

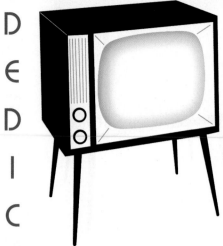

This book is dedicated first to Bob and Peg Parks, who live in Slatington, Pennsylvania, in a fabulous geodesic home. They go to flea markets and antique malls searching for new treasures. All of their great finds are displayed throughout their open-concept dwelling.

The exterior grounds of their home are lavishly landscaped with exotic trees. Interesting multi-hued geometric wood designs are shown throughout the home's interior.

I had the happy occasion to spot Bob and Peg's TV lights set up for sale in the summer of 2001. One Sunday, Carole and I visited Renninger's Outdoor Flea Market in Adamstown, Pennsylvania.

After we admired and examined the collection, a pleasant discussion began. Stories were shared, and we viewed colored photos, bound in notebooks, of their collection.

The rest is history for us, the Parks, and the collectors who have purchased this book. We trust that it will prove very helpful to you.

On Saturday and Sunday, January 19 and 20, 2002, we drove to the Parks' home to photograph their vast collection. Carole and I thank them for their help, for sharing their wonderful collection and home with us, and for their overall cordiality and interest.

While seeking information and examples for this book, the author visited flea markets, cooperatives, and auctions, used bookstores, individual shops, and the Internet, and interviewed numerous individuals.

Several avid private collectors provided valuable information and permitted access to their collections. One such person is Lynda Dawson.

By coincidence, I was searching the Internet and came upon a site called easyCollector.com. Here a collector can keep track of a collection and display it for the world. This site was created by Lynda's son, Bruce Jeschke.

Lynda had been chosen by the easyCollector.com staff as the Collector of the Month. She showed many organized collections.

To my good fortune, I discovered that she owns and enjoys a very large and diverse collection of TV lamps. She and her son agreed to share the collection for this book.

Featured are many unusual and valuable examples. I have codedicated this book to Lynda Dawson and Bruce Jeschke for their interest and assistance.

My deepest appreciation and thanks to the following:

- Mr. and Mrs. Robert Parks, Slatington, PA
- Eric Laury, Seattle, WA
- Carole Macalush, Bloomsburg, PA
- Crysta Macalush, Allentown, PA
- Kris Derbyshire, Walnutport, PA
- Martha Weimer, Allentown, PA
- Rudy P. Bitting, East Greenville, PA
- Heritage I, Adamstown, PA
- Heritage II, Reamstown, PA
- Shupp's Grove Flea Market, Adamstown, PA
- Red Mill Antiques, Bloomsburg, PA

- Earl F. Rebman, Lancaster, PA
- Moyer Stamps & Collectibles, Kutztown, PA
- Elliot Laury, Bloomsburg, PA
- Leesport Antiques Mart, Leesport, PA
- Roller Mills Marketplace, Lewisburg, PA
- Silver Moon Antique Mall, Lewisburg, PA
- Black Diamond Antiques, Frackville, PA
- Zionsville Antique Mall, Zionsville, PA
- Quaker Antique Mall, Quakertown, PA
- Lynda Dawson and Bruce Jeschke

- The two major collections shown in this book belong to Lynda Dawson and Bob and Peg Parks. Other contributors include Martha Weimer, Rudy Bitting, Eric Laury, and Carole Macalush.

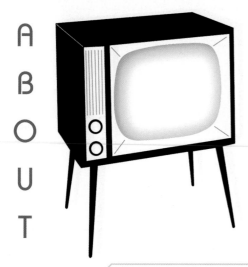

John A. Shuman III, a lifelong resident of Pennsylvania, taught secondary English for 35 years. He also taught a variety of adult courses. He avidly buys and sells, refinishes, lectures about, and appraises antiques. He enjoys photography and attending flea markets and antique shows. Shuman takes great pleasure in traveling and researching glass, china, primitives, arts and crafts, collectibles, and assorted antiques. His memberships include Smithsonian Associates, Nature Conservancy, the National Early American Glass Club, Berks County Antique Dealers' Association, National Trust for Historical Preservation, Pennsylvania State Antiques Association, Antique Appraisal Association of America, and Mount Washington Art Glass Society.

He is a graduate of Bloomsburg High School, Wyoming Seminary, Bloomsburg University, and Pennsylvania State University. He has visited renowned museums, galleries, and historical societies both in the United States and Europe. His travels have taken him to the British Isles and 16 European countries on seven occasions.

Over three decades, he has written more than 1,000 articles for the following publications: *Collectors News,* the *New York Antique Almanac,* the *Antique Trader Weekly, Antiques Journal,* the *Antique Trader Price Guide to Antiques,* the *Historical Review of Berks County,* and *Glass Collector's Digest.* He created two videos on American and European art glass for Award Video and Film Distributors (Sarasota, Florida) in 1993. He also interviews for television and radio shows. As a feature writer, his weekly column on general antiques appeared in the Sunday edition of the *West Chester Daily Local* from 1988 to 1999. Mr. Shuman also owns the Town Perk Restaurant and Cafe at 112 East Main Street in Bloomsburg, Pennsylvania, and Jasel's Antiques and Collectibles at 364 East Street, also in Bloomsburg.

TV Lamps to Light the World is Shuman's eighth book; his other titles are *A Spiritual Journey, Warman's Native American Collectibles, Art Glass Sampler, The Collector's Encyclopedia of American Art Glass, Lion Pattern Glass, The Collector's Encyclopedia of Gaudy Dutch and Welsh,* and *Art Glass — Identification and Price Guide.*

I have been collecting for many years and never knew what a TV lamp was. I collected cookie jars and Depression glass and had been in many antique stores and flea markets, and never noticed the lamps.

One day I was at a sidewalk sale in a nearby town and saw this ship lamp outside of an antique shop. I was intrigued. I thought there must be more lamps like this one, so I bought it for $7.00.

I took it home to show my husband and told him I was going to collect figural lamps. He laughed and thought I was kidding. He thought the lamp was very ugly. I assured him that I was serious and began my search for more lamps. I started coming home with more and more of these lamps.

One of the lamps was described as a TV lamp by the seller. It made sense, I guess. I started to search for more information about them. Not much could be found. I found more and more lamps as time went on.

My sister in Michigan began to look for them for me. She found several and brought them to me, with hesitation. Shortly after that, she started collecting them too. While she was looking for them for me, she fell in love with them too. We had so much fun collecting them. Our phone calls on the weekends started with, "Well, what did you get?" Now my husband loves the lamps too. He never minds if I buy another one for my collection. My collection is one of the largest in the country!

My mother and I went on several trips throughout the Midwest. She collects salts and peppers. We searched out every antique shop and mall we could find. Each year we planned out more new places to go. We would go for several days and come home and empty the car. We thought it was Christmas every time! The floor was covered with bubble wrap, newspapers, and tissue paper from our goodies. We would count how many lamps and salts and peppers we had found. We were like little kids counting their toys. Many nights in the hotel rooms, we would do the same. We both will always cherish the good times we had on our trips. I hope we have many more.

I do not remember any TV lamps from my teens. I do, however, remember one from when I was very young. My grandmother had one on her buffet table in the dining room. It was the long sleek black panther. Yes, the one that everyone remembers.

What do I know about TV lamps? I know that early in the 1950s, the average person could finally afford to buy a television. Most were paid for over time, but they were still affordable. Televisions were a big popular modern item to buy.

All we knew about this invention was that owning a TV was like having a movie theater in your home. We watched our new TV at night with the lights out, in order to see it better. The picture showed up better in the dark.

Now a scare was the gossip about watching the set in the dark. We could all ruin our eyes. How could the manufacturer remedy this awful scare? Well, someone came up with this little figural indirect light that would not shine in our eyes, but light the room to the back or toward the top of the TV set. It was the answer to saving our eyes while still allowing us to have the feeling that we were in the theater. The figural pottery, chalk ware, or metal lamp was also designated to decorate our homes. Oriental styles, horses, and many other images in vogue fit right in. Now we could watch our TV in high style and without a worry.

Many television makers gave away a TV lamp with the cost of a new television. Many other television dealers sold the lamps cheap, to ensure that we would not worry about hurting our eyes.

By the early 1960s, the television improved and showed well in any light. The big scare about ruining our eyes was not a problem anymore. I know a few TV lamps were made in the early 1960s, but not much longer. I think what is most unique about TV lamps is that they span such a short era, 1950 to 1960.

Where would a collector go to discover a TV lamp? This is another story in itself. I told you about my many trips with my mother. I also had many trips with my husband, my sister, and my wonderful kids. I was happy to find another town and antique mall. My sons and their wives helped a lot. They were always looking for a new place to go when I visited them.

I was told on many occasions that I might look on the Internet. I had absolutely no desire to learn how to use the computer. For years, my husband had one and wanted to teach me, but I had no reason. I had a close friend who wanted to teach me too. I guessed I was just too old. No reasoning could persuade me.

One day one of my sweet daughters-in-law called me and said there were 100 TV lamps on eBay. Well, that was all it took. I waited by the computer for my husband to come home from work and teach me how to turn it on. I wanted to know how to get to eBay and look at the TV lamps. Oh, what a new world I was entering. That was four years ago, and I must say, I am so proud to have learned how to use the computer. I bought many lamps that I would never have found just traveling around. I have also made many friends on the computer. People are nice wherever you go.

Over the years of collecting, I have learned not to buy glass or pottery chipped, cracked, or broken. That is a belief that I stand very firm on. When it comes to TV lamps I make one exception. I do not care if the wiring is bad. That's something that can and should be changed, if you are going to turn the lamp on and see it everyday. I have several lamps that have old wiring. I do not display my lamps turned on. Okay, one or two, but most are all together in a room on shelves. I had several outlets installed and track lighting. If I wish to plug in some of my favorites, I can show them off. I admire collectors who can display their beautiful TV lamps all over their house. I am not creative like these people. Television lamps are in demand now and will be much more so in the future. More and more people are decorating in the 1950s style. I have seen one collector take an old floor model television and place a new set in the case. A TV lamp on top of such a television would make you feel like you just stepped into the 1950s.

Each TV lamp is a conversation topic of its own. There are many lamps that can be placed nicely in any room of the house. I can see a swan or fish in the bathroom, a rooster in the kitchen, a cute cat or dog in a child's room, a pheasant in the den, and on and on. They make charming nightlights.

-Lynda Dawson

Ten years ago, if someone had told either Peg or myself that an impromptu visit to a conclave of shops dealing in antiques and collectibles would drastically alter our lifestyle, how and where we would spend our time, and even influence the way we would decorate our home, we probably would have called that person crazy.

It all began on a Sunday after church. We would usually go for a drive, stopping for dinner at a nice restaurant, or browsing through the same old, same old shopping mall. This particular Sunday during our drive, our attention was drawn to a roadside sign that read "NEXT EXIT — COLLECTORS' COVE ANTIQUES AND COLLECTIBLES."

Peg and I knew nothing about either, but our curiosity drew us into what would later become one of our favorite haunts.

Exploring the booths, Peg was attracted to a beautiful Palomino horse statue. Picking it up for examination, she noticed that it had a light socket. An elderly couple seated in the booth informed us that what we were admiring was a TV lamp from the 1950s. They also pointed out a Mallard duck lamp. Both lamps had been in their home for years. However, that day the lamps were recycled into our home. Thus began an odyssey that has taken us far and wide in search of the oftentimes elusive television lamp.

The spark was ignited. We began stopping at yard sales, searching out flea markets, and reading everything we could find concerning TV lamps.

Our collection began to grow. We were amazed at the wide variety of plants, birds, and animals that flowed from the imaginations of the myriad of manufacturers who produced these lovely additions for any room. Horses, deer, dogs, panthers, and birds of every description all had one thing in common. They had a light socket and bulb to provide backlighting atop your television.

A bit of history is probably required at this time. In the early years of television, the black and white picture was fuzzy and snowy. There was a flickering that was thought to be harmful to the viewer's vision when the picture was watched in a totally dark room.

The obvious solution to this problem was a lamp displayed on top of the television to provide backlighting and thereby ease the strain on the eyes.

A market opened for the manufacture of these lamps. Companies such as Royal Haeger, Hull, Lane of California, Maddux of California, Kron of Texas, and many others grabbed at the chance to have their creations adorn every television set in the country.

I can recall the long, sleek, black panther stalking across the console set in our living room during my teenage years.

In ten years of collecting, Peg and I have seen stately horses, running deer, gazelles, rams, poodles, pugs, hound dogs, roosters, egrets, bluebirds, cardinals, flamingoes, ballerinas, dancers, sailfish, and a wide range of fabulous panthers, leopards, cougars, elephants, and buffalo. They all said to us, "Take me home," and we did.

Unfortunately, over the past few years the supply of lamps has dwindled. At one time, a walk through an antiques mall would provide the searcher with a wide variety of lamps to choose from. Now it seems that only the same old common lamps show up. The really desirable, rare ones have gone into homes and collections.

The secret is to never give up the hunt. That lamp that you saw in a book may be lurking back on a shelf in that shop that you almost chose to ignore. Peg and I have discovered our favorites in the least likely places.

We have made it rule number one to be extremely selective in choosing a TV lamp. It has to be free of defects, especially chips. Finding a lamp in perfect condition is rough, but not impossible. We never permit dirt or even a faulty cord or socket from dissuading us. These can be remedied, where a crack or chip cannot. It takes great discipline to walk away from a lamp you really covet, because of some kind of damage. But, you can always find another — maybe.

We have made our TV lamp collection an integral part of our decor. I installed glass shelves in our living room and bedroom to display our favorites. Lamps also adorn our kitchen counters and shelves. We light them at dusk to enjoy the fruits of our labor.

Each lamp holds a memory of where we found it and has a story as to how we acquired it. I have always advised friends with children to buy them a TV lamp. It can be enjoyed, used as a nightlight, and will increase in value, becoming part of an heirloom collection. There is nothing tacky about any TV lamp that I have seen, although I will concede that "beauty is in the eyes of the beholder."

Lately it seems that anything from the 1950s is highly sought after, including television lights. That could explain why they are so difficult to find, and why they are so pricey when found.

It took a long time for people to realize what a beautiful functional item they can have when they invest in a piece of our not-too-distant past.

Peg and I enjoy watching movies from the 1950s, because every now and then you will see a Haeger horse or a Lane deer on top of a TV.

It is perhaps difficult to comprehend that many of the TV lamps that we have in our collection are already 50 years old. That explains why some persons, 30 or so years of age, may admire the beauty of each lamp, but when you explain that it is a television lamp, they have that blank expression signifying that they have no idea what you are talking about. The generation gap has never been more obvious.

Displaying any large collection poses a challenge, especially with TV lamps. Because they have to be lighted to show them off, you need to have an electrical outlet within reach. If you have shelves of lamps, you will need many receptacles.

My 46 years as an electrician have been a definite asset, enabling me to provide the electrical work needed to install multiple outlets below the display shelves.

Peggy discovered a unique problem that not even I was prepared to deal with. She would not have deer and panthers sharing the same shelf! Panthers eat deer.

Well, not wanting to incur the wrath of the animal rights people, I had to provide a shelf just for deer and another for panthers. Hopefully you will not have to face such problems with your collection. The fun of any collection is finding just the right way to show it off. People can use their own creativity to light up their homes and lives.

As with all things in life, you live and learn; so it is with collecting television lamps. We found our first Palomino horse marked plainly on the back at the socket, engraved "Lane & Company, Van Nuys, California." As our collection grew, we found lamps marked by Maddux of California and Kron of Texas. However, those lamps produced by Haeger and McCoy and Hull were not marked.

I personally feel that these companies relied on their style and glaze to set them apart. With experience, you will know at a glance whether the lamp you have found is Haeger or Hull. I have to admit that the lamps created by Royal Haeger are our favorites. The stylized forms of the race horses, with their fabulous glazes, set them apart from all others. As Peg and I go shopping, we can tell at a glance which manufacturer made a particular lamp.

I have to admit that I can only guess what TV lamps cost in the 1950s. They had to be priced right, because they found their way into the homes of most people.

Folks back then that paid five or ten or fifteen dollars would be stunned at the same lamp selling for 100 dollars or more. As with any antique or collectible, the more elaborate and rare the lamp, the higher the selling price.

Some of the lamps in our collection we have only seen one time, and had we rebelled at paying what we considered a high price, we would have missed ever having that lamp. It is sometimes a tough choice, but we have never regretted spending that extra dollar to get what we want. "If only" are two words that are difficult to swallow after walking away from a lamp that you really wanted.

Every lamp that we have either bought or sold carries with it a story. There is one episode that, although it occurred a few years ago, is still fresh in my mind. It centers around what is considered by collectors the most sought after TV lamp of them all. It is the flamingo lamp made by Land and Company.

We had searched high and low for that lamp for years, with no success. Finally, in a last ditch effort, I sent a request to *Reminisce Magazine* asking for help in locating the elusive flamingo lamp. After several weeks, we had a letter from a woman in South Carolina, informing us that she had the lamp we were after. She said if we were interested we should let her know and she would research a fair price for the lamp.

Her next letter shattered our dreams of finally adding the flamingo lamp to our collection. She related how she had taken the lamp to get it appraised. When she returned home, she attempted to enter the front doorway carrying groceries and the lamp as well. Unfortunately, the door swung shut, hitting and breaking the lamp. She offered to mail us the pieces, but we declined her offer. Many months passed before we finally found a perfect flamingo lamp from an outside dealer. That place has always been one of our favorite places to search for TV lamps.

The most rewarding part of selling is to have someone get back to you who truly loves the TV lamp that he or she purchased. On occasion, such people take time to send cards or letters telling how great their lamps look in their homes. Special events like that make selling very worthwhile.

Our fascination with television lamps has led us down many paths. Finding lamps fabricated by Royal Haeger opened the door to Haeger Pottery. As we found pieces of this pottery we added them to our collection. Then our attention was drawn to slag lamps from the 1920s. We began collecting these beautiful lamps that turn up with TV lamps in the antique malls we frequent. Peg and I both regret that we did not discover the wonderful world of collecting many years ago.

-Bob and Peg Parks

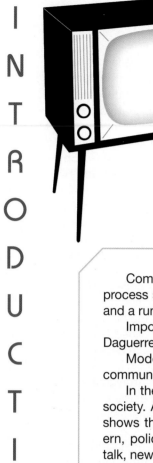

INTRODUCTION

Communication and the ability to comprehend the thoughts of others has been an ongoing process since ancient man. He utilized cave painting, clay tablets, smoke signals, the lighthouse, and a runner.

Important inventions in communication were Gutenberg's movable type, Morse's telegraph, Daguerre's camera, Bell's telephone, and Edison's phonograph.

Modern methods of communication include the radio, the television, motion pictures, the communication satellite, and the computer.

In the 1940s, television became the window on the world for a great majority of industrialized society. All forms of programming were viewed whenever a television was present. The types of shows that evolved were family and non-family situation comedy, comedy-variety, variety, western, police, detective, adventure, suspense, lawyer, spy, soap opera, hospital, quiz and game, talk, news, children's, religious, educational, and movies.

Television lamps became an integral part of this entire developmental process. TV lamps did light the world, making communication much more meaningful and enjoyable.

Today TV lamps in a vast variety of shapes and themes are highly sought and admired by collectors throughout the world. What was a passing fancy is now back in the limelight. TV lamps have reinvented themselves, and a new generation now thoroughly appreciates them. Interesting how history repeats itself.

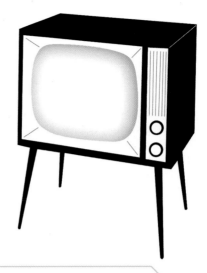

California Originals, Torrence, California

William D. Bailey began his company using the name Heirlooms of Tomorrow in 1945 in Manhattan Beach, California. Lace porcelain figurines were created that were equal to those produced by European firms.

In the 1950s the name of the company was changed to California Originals, and its location was moved to Torrence, California. Pottery art wares were produced for Montgomery Ward, JCPenney, Sears, Kmart, Disney, and Sesame Street. Other customers included S & H Green Stamps and Top Value.

The company employed around 645 people. For two years in the late 1950s, it produced for Gilner, whose firm had been destroyed by fire. California Originals purchased Gilner's molds, which included those for swan planters, figures, ashtrays, shakers, lazy susans, bowls, animals, and others.

Equipment and molds were bought by Treasure Craft. That firm has not used the molds.

Gilner

Gilner was a California firm producing in 1951. It was connected with Triangle Studios, located in El Monte and Los Angeles, California. A variety of opinions exist as to whether Gilner was a department store, an importer, a distributor, or a pottery.

Gonder Ceramic Arts, Inc., Zanesville, Ohio

G. Lawton Gonder founded Gonder Ceramic Arts, Inc., in 1941, at the Zane Pottery, formerly called Peters and Reed. Gonder had worked at Florence Pottery and American Encaustic Tile. He marketed inexpensive chain store wares and high-priced art pottery.

Gonder, an expert with ceramic glazes, was recognized by the American Ceramic Society and awarded a fellowship. Notable contributions to American ceramic arts were his flambé glazes, resembling flames streaked with yellow. Antique Gold Crackle was made successfully by Gonder, after potters had tried unsuccessfully for 2,000 years. Twenty-four karat gold was poured over the shapes, then crackled with an exclusive process. Gonder also developed "volcanic glazes." Two different glazes with different melting temperatures and chemical properties ran and melted over each other.

Gonder's best artists and sculptors included Jamie Matcher, Chester Kirk, Helen Conover, and F. F. Greene.

Interesting glazes include: Ming yellow and blue, Celadon, Gold Lustre, Gold Antique, Yellow Chinese Crackle, Mother of Pearl Lustre, Coral Lustre, White Chinese Crackle, Turquoise Chinese Crackle, Ebony Green, Royal Purple, and Wine Brown.

Haeger Potteries, Dundee, Illinois

Haeger has been in business since 1871. Now in its 130th year, its commitments are to craftsmanship, value, quality, and customer satisfaction.

German immigrant David H. Haeger founded the firm in 1871, calling it Dundee Brickyard. This firm fired millions of bricks used to build the Midwest after the great Chicago fire of 1871.

Edmund H. Haeger, one of David's sons, helped to make the transition from brickmakers to artisans. In 1900, the company was making red clay flowerpots for florists. By 1912, a sophisticated line of glazed artware was available.

J. Martin Stangl joined the Haeger staff in 1914. His designs were classical and Arts and Crafts shapes. He had worked for Fulper Pottery, a New Jersey company known for simple shapes and flowing glazes.

Edmund Haeger built a factory at the Chicago World's Fair of 1934. The Century-of-Progress fair lasted for one year, and the ceramic factory showed modern and ancient production. Some four million visitors visited the exhibit, which also featured southwestern Native American potters.

Joseph F. Estes became the general manager of Haeger in 1938. That same year, Royal Hickman joined the firm and introduced Royal Haeger. Hickman, born in Oregon in 1893, once suffered sunstroke in Panama. During his recovery, he sculpted. Art pottery historian Marion Nelson called his work for Haeger "undulating movements combined with Art Deco stylization." Royal Haeger is a favorite with collectors. Hickman left Haeger in 1944, but continued to contribute on a freelance basis. His sleek, elongated black panther was offered in three sizes in 1941.

Eric Olsen was another famous chief designer with Haeger. His career spanned 25 years (1947 – 1972). His forms include the bloodred bull.

Other sculptors and designers were Sebastiano Maglio, Sascha Brastoff, Glenn Richardson, and Franz Joseph Koenig.

In the 1940s and 1950s, inexpensive table and TV lamps were created. Some shapes featured angelfish, sleek panthers, cowboys on bucking broncos, and prospectors and their burros.

The Royal Haeger line continues to grow, and is the bestselling line of American artware. Haeger Potteries made the *Guiness Book of Records* in 1976 by creating the largest hand-thrown vase in the world. It measures more than eight feet and weighs over 650 pounds.

In 1979 Joseph F. Estes's daughter, Alexandra, became president of Haeger Potteries. In 1984 she also became president of the parent company, Haeger Industries.

Over the years Haeger production systems have been refined as to methods, materials, and scientific controls. Skilled handwork is still essential. Artwares and lamps today are perhaps superior to works produced earlier. Costs are still within the reaches of all those who have an interest in this pottery.

The manufacturing process requires the following ingredients: flint and limestone from Illinois, kaolin from Georgia and Florida, and ball clay from Tennessee and Kentucky. After these raw materials are washed and purified with water they become a smooth slip. This liquid is poured into plaster-of-Paris molds. Casting thickness is determined by the time that the mold is left standing. Then the extra slip is poured away.

After the mold is opened, the casting is permitted to dry. A finisher removes all seams and mold marks skillfully with a knife.

Next the *greenware* is sent to the drying rooms. At the end of 20 hours, the greenware is fired in a kiln for 35 hours. When this process is complete, the pieces are termed *bisque*.

Bisque examples are decorated in assorted ways — by hand, dipped, or sprayed. Compounds of powders and minerals take on fantastic colors, adding great beauty to each piece. Beautiful decoration is accomplished through the glazemaster's skills.

Finally, the glazed bisque is placed back in the kiln for another 35 hours, where it is fired at 1900 degrees. This extreme heat turns the glaze into a liquid that hardens like glass. Wondrous colors become evident, shown for the first time.

NOTABLE HAEGER DESIGNERS

SASCHA BRASTOFF — A California designer known by the well-to-do and motion picture stars in Hollywood. He was talented in numerous art forms. His art is in major art museums and examples may be acquired from his California company. In 1971 he designed a line of about 50 pieces, called Roman Bronze and Esplanade, that show Florentine and Spanish influences.

MARTIN I. DEUTSCH — A New York painter and sculptor who is credited with several designs.

ALRUN OSTERBERG GUEST — Came to Haeger from Berlin, Germany, in 1969. She graduated from Hohr-Grenzhausen, a ceramics school. At present she is a ceramics engineer at Haeger. She and her staff painted potters at work on the 1983 vase that is recognized as the largest by the *Guiness Book of Records*. This magnificent example is on display in the Haeger Museum.

ROYAL ARDEN HICKMAN — His works are free flowing, filled with both a sense of imagination and technique. He has fashioned works of art not only in pottery, but in wood, aluminum, paper, crystal, onyx, and silver.

He was born in Williamette, Oregon, in 1893, and later graduated from the Mark Hopkins Art Academy in San Francisco. During the Depression, he worked for a construction company building the Madden Dam for the Panama Canal. Sunstroke left him partially paralyzed. He strengthened his limbs and fingers in California by shaping clay. Upon recovery, he designed tableware for S. & G. Gump Co. and Garden City Pottery.

Hickman worked in Italy, Denmark, Sweden, and Czechoslovakia during Nazi occupation. He designed crystal for J. H. Vernon of New York City and for the Swedish firm Kosta Glassbruck.

In 1938 he joined Haeger Potteries. Later, as its chief designer, he created the Royal Haeger line, which proved quite successful.

Haeger constructed a second tunnel kiln to keep up with the demand for Royal Haeger. In 1939, the Royal Haeger Lamp Co. was created. A complete line of TV lamps was created, including the famous Haeger black panther that has often been imitated. Royal Hickman departed Haeger in 1944 to pursue other interests.

In the 1940s Hickman worked for Vernon Potteries, Bruce Fox Aluminum, the Heisey Glass Co., and at his own Royal Hickman Industries with branches in California; Tampa, Florida; and Chattanooga, Tennessee.

EDWIN K. KAELKE — Worked at Haeger for 50 years, first as a designer and then as executive vice-president, and general manager.

FRANZ JOSEPH KOENIG — Born in Vreeland, Netherlands, on August 14, 1882. Koenig graduated from high school and then attended the Art Institute of Haarlem. Later he graduated from the Ceramic School of Hohr-Grenzhausen, in Germany. He was the assistant manager of the Delft Corporation, in Hilversum, the Netherlands, for seven years, and owned his own pottery for five years.

He worked for the Taastrup Faience factory in Copenhagen, Denmark, in 1916. After that he was assistant manager of a factory in Wilhelmsburg, Austria.

The Bureau of Industries, Netherlands, sent him to the Dutch East Indies as ceramics consultant in 1918. Upon completion of his contract, he went to work for the Haeger Potteries.

Koenig has been a member of the American Ceramic Society since 1923. In 1924, Franz Joseph Menko Koenig served as superintendent and ceramics engineer.

SEBASTIANO MAGLIO — A seventh generation potter and a professor of art in Sicily. He started working for Haeger in 1963. His major accomplishment is throwing the world's largest art pottery vase, which was completed in December 1971.

ERIC OLSEN — Worked for Haeger for 25 years. Olsen was born in Drammen, Norway, in 1903. His art training began at age 11, in Paris, London, and Oslo. He worked in England for Spode and Wedgwood. In 1936 he was selected as the National Register designer by the English Board of Trade. He gave, in 1937, a private exhibit in London, opened by the queen of Norway. One very popular design was R-1510, his red bull, also made in ebony and mandarin orange. He has also created busts of famous people, including Carl Sandburg, Winston Churchill, and Mahatma Ghandi. At the 100th anniversary of Haeger Pottery, Olsen's memorial bust of Edmund H. Haeger was unveiled. It is on display at the Macomb and Dundee, Illinois plants.

C. GLENN RICHARDSON — Began as director of design in 1971. He has studied at San Diego Junior College, Wright Junior College, and the Illinois Institute of Design. He has designed for the U.S. Marines.

LEE SECRIST — Studied art in Florence, Italy; the Yale School of Fine Arts; the Chicago Art Institute; and the Chicago Academy of Fine Arts. He was hired to supervise and design for Haeger in 1946. His work includes artware and pieces for the lamp company in Macomb.

MARTIN J. STANGL — Began to develop a commercial artware line for Haeger in 1914, and worked for the company for five years. He returned to Fulper as general manager in 1920. Later he started Stangl Pottery, well known for its line of colorful birds. Some special pieces of Haeger are signed "J. Stangl."

OTHER POPULAR DESIGNERS — Ben Seibel, Elaine Douglas Carlock, A. H. Estes, Maria Fuchs, Elsa Ken Haeger, Don Lewis, Kathryn DeSousa, Kevin Bradley, Helen Conover, Helmut Bruchmann, and many others.

HAEGER CATALOG OFFERINGS

The following are TV lamp prices set by Haeger during the 1954 – 1956 period. Prices listed were retail values and were "subject to customary discount."

Spring 1954
- 6202 Greyhound — Platinum Grey, Ebony, Mahogany, Catseye; 10¼" high, $8.50.
- 6191 Flare — Sunset Yellow, Catseye, Chartreuse/Honey, Ebony; 5" high, $5.50.
- 6140 Sailfish — Catseye, Platinum Grey/White, Oxblood/White, Chartreuse/Honey; 8½" high, $7.00.
- 6200 Gazelle — Catseye, Ebony, Walnut/White, Mahogany/White; 10½" high, $8.50.
- 5353 Petal Louvre — Chartreuse/Honey, Green Agate, Oxblood/Honey, Cotton White, Walnut; 11½" high, $12.00.
- 6193 Colt TV Planter — Ebony, Mahogany/White, Catseye, Walnut/White; 13½" high, $13.50.
- 6198 Gondola — Green Agate with Chartreuse Plastic Shield, Ebony with Red Plastic Shield; 7¼" high, $15.00.
- 6044 Prancing Horse — Chartreuse, Green Agate; 11" high, $13.50.
- 6116 Acanthus — Green Agate, Chartreuse/Honey, Platinum Grey, Oxblood/Honey; 7" high, $9.00.
- 5415 Gazelle TV Planter — Green Agate, Walnut/Decorated, Ebony/Decorated; 14" high, $21.00.
- 6124 Fish — Green Agate, Chartreuse/Honey, Platinum Grey/Decorated, Oxblood/Honey; 13½" high, $12.00.
- 5473 Deer Abstract — Green Agate, Oxblood/Honey, Chartreuse/Honey; 15¼" high, $15.50.
- Pagoda TV Planter — Ebony/Chartreuse, Oxblood/White, Dark Green/Chartreuse; 10" high, $13.50.
- Double Colt — Green Agate, Oxblood and Chartreuse with White Glasschop shade; 26" high, $25.00.

Spring 1955
- 6322 Ocean Fantasy — Green Agate, Turquoise Green/Decorated, Haeger Red/Decorated; 21½" high, $8.75.
- 6200 Gazelle — Catseye, Ebony, Briar/White; 14½" long, 10" high, $4.25.

- 6341 Cocker Figurine — Briar/Decorated, Cotton White, Mat Black; 10½" high, $4.50.
- 6356 Poodle — Cotton White, Mat Black, Briar/Decorated; 10½" high, $4.50.
- 6256 Pagoda TV Planter — Ebony/White, Turquoise Green/Decorated, Ebony, Dark Green/White; 11¼" high, 12½" long, $5.00.
- 6198 Gondola — Green Agate with Chartreuse Plastic Shield, Ebony with Red Plastic Shield; 9" high, 19½" long, $7.50.
- 6301 Freeform Lantern TV Planter — Ebony, Catseye, Turquoise Green/Decorated; 12" high, 11½" wide, $5.00.
- 6357 Boxer — Briar/Decorated, 10½" high, $4.50.
- 6202 Greyhound — Platinum Grey, Ebony, Catseye; 7½" high, 12½" long, $4.25.
- 6289 Bell Flower — Ebony, Catseye; 13" high, $5.00.
- 5353 Petal Louvre — Green Agate, Cotton White, Turquoise Green/Decorated; 11½" high, $5.00.
- 6261 Double Horse — Catseye, Ebony, Briar/White; 10½" high, $4.25.
- 6263 Globe Reflector — Ebony, Dark Green, Mat White; 9½" high, $3.50.

Fall 1955
- 6375 Centaur with Bow — Mint Green/Decorated, Mat Black, Turquoise Green/Decorated; 16½" high, $13.50.
- 6376 Aquaria — Mint Green/Decorated, Turquoise Green/Decorated, Haeger Red with Plastic Shield; 13½" high, $11.50.
- 6373 Oriental Sampan Planter TV — Ebony with Yellow Figure and Planter, Turquoise Green/Decorated with Glass White Figure and Planter; 14½" high, $17.50.
- 6377 Sun Fish — Turquoise Green/Decorated, Mint Green/Decorated, Haeger Red; 17½" high, $10.00.
- 6379s Urn — Mat White, Sandalwood Crackle, Haeger Red (White Liner); 11" high, $10.00.
- 6374 Town Crier Lantern — Mat Black, Cinna Brown, Patina Green; 14½" high, $10.00.

Fall Supplement 1956
- 6475 Small Bull — Haeger Red; 11" high.
- 6477 Wild Horses — Ebony/Decorated Antique; 16" high.
- 6478 Dachshund — Briar/Decorated; 10½" high.
- 6479 Scottie — Mat Black/Decorated; 10½" high.
- 6480 Collie — Briar/Decorated, 10½" high.
- 6472 Comedy & Tragedy — Ebony/Decorated, Saffron/Decorated, Turquoise Green/Decorated; 7½" high.
- 6473 Fish Shadow Box — Turquoise Green/Decorated, Mat Black, Saffron/Decorated; 11" high.
- 6474 Ballet Dancers — Turquoise Green/Decorated, Mat Black, Saffron/Decorated; 8" high.

Permanent Displays
- Chicago — 1574 Merchandise Mart
- Portland — J.C. Simmons, Rm. 315, Fitzpatrick Building, 917 Oak Street
- Dallas — Mack Higginbothom, 335 Second Unit, Santa Fe Building
- New York — Harry L. Kramer, 225 Fifth Avenue, the Haeger Potteries, Inc.
- San Francisco — D.E. Sanford Co., Inc., 12th and Howard Streets
- Los Angeles — D.E. Sanford Co., Inc., 1049 Hill Street
- Toronto — Brooks Lamp & Shade, Ltd.. 44 – 50 Lombard Street

Hedi Schoop

Hedi Schoop studied fashion design, sculpture, and architecture in Berlin and Vienna. She left Nazi Germany in 1933 with her husband. He was the famous composer Frederick Holander.

The pair settled in North Hollywood, California. Hedi Schoop Creations was incorporated in 1942; it made popular novelty gift items. Many California companies copied Schoop's work.

Schoop's pieces feature hand painting, gold trim, applied ribbons, and sgraffito. She modeled both animal and human figures. Some were done in matching pairs. Most of her work is marked.

In the mid-1950s she introduced a line of TV lamps, highly sought after by collectors. A fire in 1958 closed the plant. Hedi also designed for other firms.

Schoop figures, figurines, and lamps are detailed and rich with color.

Hollywood Ceramics Company, Hollywood, California

Hollywood Ceramics Company was a manufacturing firm for Maddux of California. It produced dimestore novelties in the 1940s and 1950s. Typical glazes include bright red, maroon, dark green, and chartreuse yellow. Examples may be found unsigned or marked "Hollywood Ceramics — Made in California" or "Hollywood Ceramics."

Maddux, Los Angeles, California

Harry William Maddux was born May 1, 1917, in Vallejo, California. While in his teens he began manufacturing pottery. Before he was 20 years of age, he had three people working for him. Some of his early work is marked "William Maddux."

He married in 1938, and around 1940 opened a plant at 3020 Fletcher Drive, Los Angeles. At peak operation the firm had 15 employees and was called Valley Vista Pottery. Most pieces were hand signed and had hand-wrought flowers.

The facility was eventually sold. Bill had partners and quarrels arose between them. The name "Maddux of California" survived under several ownerships. Thus, there is a wide variety in the products offered as premiums by S & H Green Stamps and others.

Bill opened a new business in a small existing plant near Griffith Park in the Los Angeles area. The operation was called the Rembrandt Pottery, and it operated from the early 1950s through 1957.

Workers recall removing mold marks from greenware at 35 cents an hour. Many Rembrandt items had pastel and light colors sprayed with gold spotting. Maddux created, imported, and distributed ceramics and supplied chain stores throughout the country. His pieces were listed in all major stamp catalogs in the mid-1960s.

Marcia Ceramics of California, Los Angeles, California

This Los Angeles firm commenced operation about 1940. It was a family-run business. In the early 1980s two sons, Gerald and Michael Siegal, and their father ran the business.

McCoy, Roseville, Ohio

W. Nelson McCoy entered the pottery business in 1848 in Putnam, Ohio. The local trade purchased stoneware crocks and other utilitarian pieces. As the pottery improved in quality, flatboats took it down the Ohio and Mississippi rivers and distributed it to wholesale buyers.

J. W. McCoy, son of W. Nelson McCoy, founded the J. W. McCoy Pottery on September 5, 1899, in Roseville, Ohio. This firm had great success, making stoneware, pedestals, jardiniers, and larger pieces. The firm tried to make artwares similar to those made by Rookwood and Welter.

In 1910, J. W. McCoy and his son formed the Nelson McCoy Sanitary Stoneware Company. When George Brush bought into the firm in 1911, the name was changed to the Brush-McCoy Pottery Company. The partnership lasted until 1925, when the McCoys sold their interests and the name changed to the Nelson McCoy Pottery Company.

Chase Enterprises purchased the firm in 1967 and sold it in 1974 to Lancaster Colony Corporation. The business was owned by Designer Accents of Sebring, Ohio, in 1991 and went by the name Nelson McCoy Ceramics. The business no longer exists.

Treasure Craft, Compton, California

Alfred A. Levin founded Treasure Craft in Gardenia, California, in 1945. It is one of the few companies still creating cookie jars today on a large scale. The original pottery operated from a single-car garage equipped with a 15-cubic-foot kiln.

The company is now in Compton, California, and employs between 500 and 600 people. It is housed in a 250,000-square-foot building. Pfaltzgraff Pottery of York, Pennsylvania, acquired the firm in 1988.

Wahpeton Pottery Company (Rosemeade)

This firm had its beginnings in 1940. Robert J. Hughes, president, and Laura A. Taylor, secretary, treasurer, and designer, started the firm. In 1943 the two were married. Their firm's product, Rosemeade, was made in a shed at the Globe-Gazette Printing Company. The couple moved the business to a new location in 1944.

Howard Lewis was hired as manager in 1944. He had worked as a ceramic engineer at Niloak. He is credited not only with the formulation of all the glazes, but also with creating the swirl pieces, which are very collectible.

Laura Taylor's interest in wildlife is reflected in her animal shapes, ashtrays, figurines, shakers, and others pieces. Glazing occurs in solid colors and naturalistic hand-painted colors.

Laura Hughes passed away in 1959. The pottery closed in 1961, but the salesroom was kept open until 1964.

Examples are stamped in blue and black or marked with a paper label.

TV LAMP DISTRIBUTION FACTS

- A lamp was sometimes given as a promotional premium when a TV set was purchased.
- TV lamps were offered as prizes at fairs and carnivals.
- TV lamps could often be purchased on a club plan for 50¢ per week.
- A lamp was sometimes offered as a "big prize" on punch boards at service stations.
- Lamps were marketed by florists, gift shops, and chain stores.
- Lamps were sold at Sears, Montgomery Ward, Woolworth's, Kresge, Newberries, Strawbridge and Clothier, Leh and Company, Roth's Furniture Store, Home Furnishing Store, and a great variety of other stores throughout the country.
- TV lamps could be purchased with stamps from S & H Green Stamp stores, Gold Bond Gift Books, and Top Value Stamps redemption stores.
- Lamps sold for $3.69 and up.
- Earl F. Rebman Co., a well established and reputable Lancaster, Pennsylvania firm, has been in business for many years. It has two stores in Lancaster, at 1775 Columbia Avenue and 800 South Queen Street. The stores once sold TV lamps. When interviewed, Earl Jr. recalled his father waking him up early in the morning when he was fourteen. They would journey to a warehouse in Philadelphia and pick up the lamps. The firm kept all of its catalogs on record; unfortunately, a fire in the 1980s destroyed them.
- William Thomas Grant, born in 1876, opened his first W. T. Grant store in Lynn, Massachusetts. The year was 1906, and the store was situated in a YMCA. All merchandise sold for less than 25 cents, a compromise between F. W. Woolworth's 5 and 10 cent stores and the 50 cent minimum set by department stores of that day. After World War I the price cap was raised to a dollar, and it was discontinued by 1940. Grant's demise was in 1972; he was 96 years of age. His chain covered 43 states with 1,190 stores and brought in $1.5 million in yearly sales. Ames Department Stores purchased the W. T. Grant Company in 1985.
- By the 1950s, numerous regional stamps were being issued under such names as Top Value, King Korn, Blue Chip, Gift House, Gold Bond, Plaid Stamps, Triple-S, and others.
- S & H Green Stamps was founded in 1896 and was marketed nationwide. Each stamp had a cash value of ⅒ of one cent. One stamp was given for each ten cents spent.
- S & H Green Trading Stamps was founded by Thomas A. Sperry, a silverware salesman in Jackson, Michigan, and Shelly B. Hutchinson, a Michigan businessman.
- The first "premium parlor" (redemption center) opened in a small store in Bridgeport, Connecticut. Quality name brands were shown.
- Green Trading stamps were offered by grocers, dry goods dealers, department stores, gas stations, drug stores, movies, feed mills, and undertakers.
- By the late 1950s and early 1960s, trading stamps were part of the American culture.
- In 1964 S & H printed 32 million catalogs (Ideabooks) and 140 million savers books, and redeemed one billion stamps per week.
- Large numbers of Green Stamp books were collected throughout the community by schools, churches, and other non-profit organizations. Using the "Group Savings Project" they were able to purchase automobiles, needed equipment, and larger-scaled items.
- Curt Carlson borrowed $50 in 1938, printed up stamps, and began a business called Gold Bond Stamps. By 1993, his empire had grown to $11 billion.
- King Korn Stamps was started by Chicago businessman Peter Volid in 1953. Thriftway stores in the Midwest were the first to invest.
- Grand Union, a New England chain, started Triple-S (Stop & Save Stamps) in 1955.
- JCPenney and Montgomery Ward stores carried a variety of Haeger pottery.
- Pottery catalogs issued by Haeger over the years suggested that the company's TV lamps be used on portable and console model televisions, and that they could also provide light on fireplace mantels.
- Sebastian S. Kresge, a Pennsylvania Dutchman, grew up in Kresgeville in Monroe County. In 1899 Kresge started his first five- and-ten-cent store in Detroit.
- Kresge worked 20-hour days six days of the week. By 1912, S.S. Kresge Company had the second largest group of ten-cent stores in the world. The leader in the industry was Frank Woolworth, who invented the dime store.
- Kresge's successor was Harry B. Cunningham, who made the company into Kmart, a discount giant. The first Kmart was opened near Detroit in 1962.
- Kresge died in 1966, after serving as chairman of the board for 53 years. His company had been on the New York Stock Exchange all that time.
- In 1965, Kresge stores generated $850 million in business.

TV LAMP MANUFACTURING FACTS

- There were in excess of 75 manufacturers of TV lamps in the U.S.
- Most firms were located in California, while others operated in Illinois, Ohio, and Wisconsin.
- Lamps were made in greased wooden, plaster-of-Paris, and metal molds.
- Talented artisans carved the sharp and detailed originals in wood, and also molded precise clay models.
- Lamps were created in china, fine porcelain, plaster, and soapstone.
- Additions of wood, brass, stainless steel, tin, chrome, fiberglass, pressed glass flowers, and clear glass blocks were often used to decorate TV lamps. Plastic flowers were also sometimes added. Originals are difficult to find.
- Themes covered a host of ideas, with major stylistic emphasis upon modem art, Art Nouveau, and Art Deco.
- A host of glazes included high gloss, gloss, and satin.
- The durable paints were thickly applied by dipping, brushing, airbrushing, or a combination of these.
- Airbrushing details required a steady, quick hand. Blending and overlapping called for much skill.
- Stencils were fabricated from metals and plastic. These stencils had to be cleaned frequently so that they did not spoil the work previously accomplished.
- Some animals possess colorful jeweled eyes (rhinestone, marble, etc.).
- Backdrops may consist of fiberglass and glass panels in assorted colors.
- Generally, plaster-of-Paris TV lamps have round or scalloped bases. They measure ½" – 1" in thickness and often have backdrops. Painted coral and a variety of shells are often embedded perpendicularly into the base. The overall look might be enhanced with pressed plastic three-dimensional salmon flamingos with yellow beaks and legs. Also seen are swordfish, and paper labels might read "Souvenir of Florida," "Atlantic City," etc. These tourist lamps were lighted with blue, red, and white Christmas candle bulbs. Some are ink stamped on their bases with a number. Some have colorful crushed coral embedded in their plaster backdrops.

TYPICAL THEMES

For identification purposes, TV lamps have been grouped according to general collecting themes. Words and letters in parentheses indicate that the object has been seen alone and in groups. Examples: Siamese cat(s), Gondola (with Gondolier).

ART NOUVEAU, ART DECO, MODERN ART

BIRDS & BUTTERFLIES – Chinese Pheasants, Cardinals, Bluebirds, Swan(s), Owl(s), Dove(s), Parrot(s), Cockatoo(s), Rooster (and Hen), Pheasant, Flamingos, Blackbird, Crane, Peacock, Egret, Bluejay, Duck(s), Duck with Baby, Canadian Geese, Butterflies.

CATS – Cat in a Basket, Cat on a Pillow, Cat with Paw Lifted, Fat Cats, Siamese Cat(s).

DANCE, MUSIC & THEATRE – Dancer(s), Fancy Dancer, Egyptian Dancers, Ballet Dancers, Square Dancers, African Dancers, Musicians, Accordion, Lawrence Welk Accordion, Ballerina, Jack Jumping Over the Candlestick, Carousel, Victorian Couple at the Piano, Violin, Pan, Fan, Masks.

DEER – Deer, Fawn, Deer with a Fawn, Double/Triple Deer, Reindeer, Gazelle.

DOGS – Afghan Hound(s), Poodle and Lady's Head, Greyhound, Scottie, Puppy, Puppies in a Box, Two Puppies, Bulldog(s), Hunting Dog, Collie, Boxer, Yorky, Dachshund, Cocker Spaniel, Basset Hound, Toy Poodle, German Shepherd.

FLOWERS, LEAVES & FRUITS – Sunflower, Tulip, Flower, Ivy, Cornucopia, Corner Tree(s), Leaf, Handled Cornucopia Basket, Three-leaf Clover, Tree Trunk, Vine, Branches.

FRONTIER & WESTERN – Stagecoach, Covered Wagon, Elaborate Coach with People and Horses, Wagon Wheel, Cowboy on a Bucking Bronco, Cowboy Boots/Saddle, Cowboy on Horseback, Horse with a Saddle, Native American Riding a Deer, Indian Man, Trains, Buffalo, Mountain Goat.

HORSES – Stallion Head, Racehorse(s), Pony, Circus Horse, Two/Three Horse Heads.

JUNGLE – Panther(s), Pumas, Spartan with Cougar, African King, African Queen, African Royalty Head, African Head, Zulu Mask, Harem Head, Elephant, Zebra, Giraffes.

MATADORS & BULLS – Brahma Bull, Bull, Matador (Fighting a Bull).

MISCELLANEOUS – Tower of Pisa, Basket, Vases, Planters, Urns, Kerosene Lamp, Grinding Mill, Fireplace, Pitcher and Bowl, Aladdin Lamp, TV with Two Planters, Pink Globe, Lady witha Hat, Victorian Lady (and Gentleman), Toby Jug (Men and Women), Assorted TV Lamps/Clocks, Mount Rushmore Heads, Female nude, Colonial Couple, Clowns, Comedy and Tragedy Masks, Burro with a Basket, Donkey (with a Cart), Squirrel, Rabbit, Frog, Teddy Bear.

MOTION LAMPS (wide range of subjects)

ORIENTAL – Chinese Boat/Sail, Oriental Boat (with Figures), Oriental Girl on a Bridge, Oriental Lady Standing by a Gate, Oriental Man with a Basket, Oriental Girl with a Fan, Oriental Lady, Oriental Couple, Oriental Wave, Oriental House, Oriental Man (and Woman), Oriental Arbor, Dragon, Oriental Fan.

RELIGIOUS – Religious Themes, Bust of Christ, Madonna (with Child), Nun.

SEASHORE – Swordfish, Dolphin, Boy on a Dolphin, Seaweed, Angelfish, Blowfish, Aquariums, Sailfish.

SHIPS – Pirate Wave, Boat, Riverboat, Gondola (with Gondolier), Sea Nymph, Seashell, Beach Scene, Cloud, Ocean Wave, Sailboats, Lighthouse, Mermaid, Paddlewheel, Pirate Ship, Feathers, Hawaiian Woman in Canoe.

TRANSPORTATION – Cinderella Coach, Open Convertible, Twin Bicycle Riders.

Colorful airbrushed butterfly on a green base, 9" wide, $75.00 – 85.00.

Brown high-glazed rooster, 8" wide, 11½" high, $75.00 – 85.00.

Shiny dark green rooster, 10" wide, circa 1950s, $75.00 – 85.00.

Airbrushed rooster along fence, 13" wide, 12" high, signed "Lane & Co., Van Nuys, Cal., Patent Pending, #2," $100.00 – 110.00.

White rooster with gold tints, 9" wide, ceramic, $75.00 – 85.00.

Airbrushed rooster and hen, with original packaging, 12" wide, marked "Made in USA E-21855-M," $125.00 – 135.00.

Orange and other hues 1950s rooster, signed "Maddux of Calif 8014 USA," $75.00 – 90.00.

White rooster with airbrushed colors, 11½" wide, 14½" high, marked "Lane and Co.," $125.00 – 135.00.

Brown mottled swan, 9½" wide, 11" high, $95.00 – 110.00.

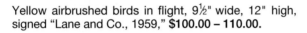

Yellow airbrushed birds in flight, 9½" wide, 12" high, signed "Lane and Co., 1959," $100.00 – 110.00.

Large airbrushed mallard duck taking flight, with planter, 13" wide, 17" high, marked "Kron," $125.00 – 135.00.

Lustered double swan, 12" wide, 7" high, $80.00 – 90.00.

Airbrushed owl, 5½" wide, 10" high,
signed "Marcia, Calif.," $75.00 – 85.00.

Quizzical airbrushed parrot, 9" wide, 9½" high,
marked "Van Nuys, Calif 1959 USA," $60.00 –
70.00.

Three airbrushed mauve quail, 11" wide,
11½" high, marked "Maddux Calif USA
8016," $100.00 – 110.00.

Pair of bluebirds, 13½" wide, 10½" high,
marked "Lane Van Nuys, Calif. 1959,"
$75.00 – 85.00.

Exotic and fancy airbrushed Japanese bird in flight, 12" wide, 9½" high, **$75.00 – 85.00.**

Colorful pair of pink cardinals, gray ground, 10" wide, 9½" high, **$55.00 – 65.00.**

Little white swan, 8" wide, 6" high, ceramic, **$60.00 – 70.00.**

Colorful ring-necked pheasant in flight, 10" wide, 9" high, **$125.00 – 135.00.**

Two-tone yellow duck, 9½" wide, 9½" high, $85.00 – 95.00.

Vibrant roadrunner, airbrushed, 9½" wide, 9½" high, marked "Maddux of Calif 60838 USA.," $85.00 – 95.00.

Maddux mallard duck, 12" wide, 11½" high, $65.00 – 75.00.

Airbrushed mallard duck, 10" wide, 9" high, ceramic, $70.00 – 80.00.

Light green Norfleet pair of doves, front planter, 13½" wide, 9½" high, marked "Norfleet, Calif.," $65.00 – 90.00.

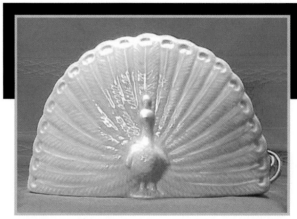

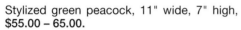

Stylized green peacock, 11" wide, 7" high, $55.00 – 65.00.

Maddux mallard duck, 12" wide, 12" high, marked "Maddux of Calif.," ornate brass base, $75.00 – 90.00.

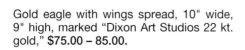

Gold eagle with wings spread, 10" wide, 9" high, marked "Dixon Art Studios 22 kt. gold," $75.00 – 85.00.

White tropical bird with spread tail, 11" wide, 13" high, **$75.00 – 90.00.**

Green and white airbrushed swan, 9½" wide, 7½" high, **$75.00 – 90.00.**

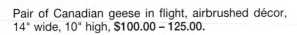

Unusual looking pheasant in flight, 10" wide, 7" high, signed "Waces, Made in Japan," **$85.00 – 95.00.**

Pair of Canadian geese in flight, airbrushed décor, 14" wide, 10" high, **$100.00 – 125.00.**

Yellow-green eagle on a dark log, 14" wide, 11" high, **$70.00 – 80.00.**

Pair of chalk white doves, ceramic, 13" wide, 10" high, **$70.00 – 80.00.**

Lime green and gold peacocks with spread tails, 12" wide, 11" high, marked "Royal Fleet, Calif., **$65.00 – 75.00.**

White Maddux swan, 1950s, 9½" wide, 12½" high, signed "Maddux of Calif.," #848, **$55.00 – 65.00.**

White double swans with airbrushed highlights, 12" wide, 10" high, marked "Maddux of Calif #825," $65.00 – 70.00.

Graceful white swan, 9" wide, 9" high, signed "Enchanto Co., Calif.," $55.00 – 65.00.

Glossy black swans with gold spatterings, 13" wide, 9½" high, signed "Kron – USA," $55.00 – 60.00.

Petite white and gold swan, 1950s, 8" wide, 9" high, wings light, $75.00 – 85.00.

White and gray Maddux double swans, with original packaging, 12" wide, 10" high, **$90.00 – 100.00.**

White swan with pink and green hints, 9½" wide, 12½" high, signed "Maddux of Calif., #828 1959," **$85.00 – 100.00.**

Snow white Lane swan, 10" wide, 12" high, **$75.00 – 85.00.**

Mallard duck taking flight, sits on a metal stand, 11" wide, 13" high, **$75.00 – 85.00.**

Airborne Maddux mallard duck, brass stand, 11" wide, 14½" high, marked "Maddux of Calif. #833 1959," $75.00 – 85.00.

Ceramic mallard duck, 10½" wide, 11½" high, $65.00 – 70.00.

Airbrushed mallard in flight, vibrant, 12" wide, 12" high, $65.00 – 75.00.

Airbrushed pheasant in flight, varied hues, mounted on a brass base, 11" wide, 13" high, signed "Maddux of Calif. E-21855-M 1959," $100.00 – 125.00.

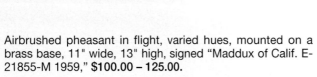

Yellow airbrushed butterfly with black and gold tints, 12" wide, 10" high, $85.00 – 95.00.

Pair of pink cockatoos with spread wings, 11" wide, 11" high, signed "Maddux of Calif. 826 M59 USA.," $125.00 – 135.00.

Burgundy and white swan, 10" wide, 7½" high, $65.00 – 75.00.

Large light pink and gold rooster with tail furled, 11½" wide, 16" high, $85.00 – 95.00.

Variegated airbrushed Maddux mallard duck, 9" wide, 10" high, fully signed "E-21855 Maddux of California 836 Made in USA.," **$80.00 – 90.00.**

Whimsical mallard duck with baby; tan, green, white, and yellow; 10½" wide, 10" high, **$100.00 – 110.00.**

Gold and white Royal Haeger ceramic rooster, 10" wide, 13" high, marked "Royal Haeger R-1897 USA," **$110.00 – 135.00.**

Seven busy variegated parrots, lightswitch is on the side, 9" wide, 9½" high, signed "Holland Mold," **$100.00 – 125.00.**

Airburshed rooster displaying pink, yellow, light green, and dark green, 11½" wide, 10" high, **$100.00 – 125.00.**

Lane green swan, wings raised, neck arched, 9½" wide, 11" high, marked "Van Nuys, Calif.," **$85.00 – 95.00.**

Lime and light green dove on a base, 10" wide, 8" high, **$75.00 – 90.00.**

Unusual light aqua double school owls, 8" wide, 9¾" high, **$100.00 – 115.00.**

Proud colorful rooster against a black wagon wheel, 11" wide, 12" high, **$100.00 – 125.00.**

Shaded and airbrushed bird, wings spread, perched on a log, 13" wide, 10" high, signed "Cali-Co.," **$75.00 – 85.00.**

Airbrushed multicolored Chinese pheasant, on a green and white base, sits in a brass holder, 11½" wide, 11½" high, signed "Maddux of Calif.," **$100.00 – 115.00.**

Airbrushed pink and white cockatoo, black beak and claws, tan and green backdrop, 9½" wide, 10" high, **$100.00 – 110.00.**

Green, black, and antique white rooster by "Lane & Co. Van Nuys Calif © 1961," Art Deco feathers, rust comb, marked with a paper foil label, airbrushed, 12" wide, 15" high, **$100.00 – 125.00.**

Red flambé rooster; bright green comb, beak, and feet; double planter, backlighted, unsigned Royal Haeger, 10" wide, 13" high, **$100.00 – 125.00.**

Fawn-shaded stylized rooster silhouetted against a rising sun, unsigned Haeger, green highlights, back planter and light, 9" wide, 14" high, **$100.00 – 125.00.**

Large airbrushed mallard duck, front dish, backlighted, marked "Lane & Co. Van Nuys Calif — © 1954," 14" wide, 15" high, **$100.00 – 125.00.**

Mallard duck, light blue and pink wings, removable brass base, stamped "E-21855-M," backlighted, front dish planter, 11½" wide, 11½" high, **$80.00 – 100.00.**

Small mallard flying duck, signed "Lane," sprayed with airbrush finish, front dish, 10" wide, 11½" high, **$50.00 – 65.00.**

Flying mallard duck in shades of moss/hunter green; other hues are charcoal black, chocolate brown, cream and chamois gold; front dish planter, backlighted, 11¼" wide, 13" high, marked "341 2N6014 © LANE & Co. Van Nuys, Calif U.S.A. 1954-1958," **$100.00 – 125.00.**

Large flying mallard duck, highly glazed, multicolored hues, full front planter, airbrushed, 14" wide, 15" high, **$100.00 – 125.00.**

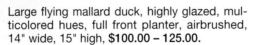

Iridescent snow white crested peacock with gilded highlights, over 50 jewels set in the tail, lights internally, marked "HOLLAND © MOLD," $85.00 – 100.00.

Large pair of pink, white, and black flamingos; backlighted, green and yellow front candy dish, signed "Lane & Co. Van Nuys, Calif. © 1957," 15" wide, 14" high, $335.00 – 350.00.

Gilded malachite double plaster-of-Paris front planter, lemon yellow swans, back fiberglass light green shade, marked "© L.M. FIELACK — DO NOT USE OVER 25 W.," $115.00 – 130.00.

Pink swan with multicolored silk-wrapped flowers, two bulbs, 13" wide, 19" high, $75.00 – 90.00.

Antique white curled neck swan, light, and planter; signed "#828 © 59 CALIF. USA," 9" wide, 12" high, **$55.00 – 75.00.**

Pearlized cream swan; mauve-tipped wings, base, and waves in Persian blue; signed "Maddux Cal.," backlighted, rear planter, 10" wide, 12" high, **$85.00 – 100.00.**

Blue-green unmarked Haeger swan, uplighted, 9" wide, 13" high, **$125.00 – 150.00.**

Royal Haeger pearl-drip glaze swan, 9" wide, 13" high, **$125.00 – 150.00.**

Three-color parrot, wired white and gilded pressed-glass flowers, 8½" wide, 10" high, **$65.00 – 75.00.**

Mother and baby swans, mauve wings tipped with black, teal waves, backlighted, back planter, 12" wide, 10" high, marked "E-21855-M," **$75.00 – 85.00.**

Colorful ring-necked pheasant in flight on a brass base, double back planter, airburshed naturalistic colors, marked "Maddux of Calif Made in USA E-21855-M 827," 11" wide, 12½" high, **$125.00 – 150.00.**

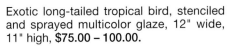

Exotic long-tailed tropical bird, stenciled and sprayed multicolor glaze, 12" wide, 11" high, **$75.00 – 100.00**.

Nutmeg-shaded mallard duck, green and tan drippings, backlighted, double planter, 17" wide, 9" high, **$85.00 – 100.00**.

Seafoam green double flying geese, gray base with cattails, four cuts in back under the light, 14" wide, 10" high, **$85.00 – 100.00**.

White airbrushed horned owl, eyes light, marked "Kron of Tex.," 10" wide, 12" high, **$100.00 – 125.00.**

Multi-tan, brown, and gray horned owl, backlighted, amber eyes that light, marked "KRON of Tex.," 10" wide, 12" high, **$100.00 – 125.00.**

Nutmeg and white owl, open eyes that light, 10" wide, 12" high, signed "Texans, Inc. Bangs, Texas" (printed on the felt), **$100.00 – 125.00.**

Purple and cream/brown young double ducklings, on blue-green porcelain driftwood, "Maddux of Calif © 59," 12" wide, 9" high, **$125.00 – 150.00.**

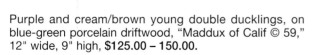

Sprayed spinach green tipped swan, black beak and eyes, slits in the wings for light, 11" wide, 9" high, **$85.00 – 100.00.**

Double bluejays on a branch, cobalt blue, light yellow on the underside of the wings, raised light pink roses on green grass, 6" wide, 9½" high, backlighted, **$65.00 – 75.00.**

Perched double bluebirds, signed "Lane and Co., Van Nuys, Cal.," 14" wide, 11" high, **$100.00 – 135.00.**

Glossy airbrushed green arched-neck swan, 22-karat gold highlights, lighted internally, 20 slits in each wing, 8" wide, 9½" high, **$85.00 – 100.00.**

Rare, glossy, coal black open-winged hovering butterfly above a large six-petal flower, vivid gold highlights, magnificent detail and design, signed "® KRON," 8" wide, 12½" high, **$225.00 – 250.00.**

Close-up of the butterfly.

C
A
T
S

Pair of airbrushed Claes reclining Siamese cats, 12" wide, 6½" high, circa 1950s, $230.00 – 240.00.

Cinnamon brown Spartan with cougar, white decorative shield, 15" wide, 8" high, $65.00 – 75.00.

Tan and black cat with paw raised, 8½" wide, 11" high, $225.00 – 235.00.

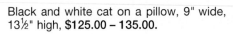

Black and white cat on a pillow, 9" wide, 13½" high, $125.00 – 135.00.

Airbrushed black and white fat cats, 9½" wide, circa 1954, Claes, $125.00 – 135.00.

Single airbrushed Siamese cat, 6½" wide, $75.00 – 85.00.

Three black and white airbrushed cats with marble eyes that light up, 12" wide, $100.00 – 110.00.

Shiny black cats, rhinestone eyes, 9" wide, 11½" high, $75.00 – 85.00.

Pair of black and white airbrushed cats with a black basket, 9" wide, 11" high, $75.00 – 85.00.

Pair of airbrushed black and white Siamese cats, rhinestone eyes, 12" wide, 13" high, $75.00 – 85.00.

Siamese black and white cat family, airbrushed, rhinestone eyes, 15" wide, 13" high, marked "Kron," $85.00 – 100.00.

Pensive and furry white cat, 9" wide, 10" high, circa 1950s, $75.00 – 90.00.

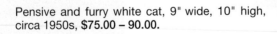

Elongated Siamese single cat, black and white, 6" wide, 10½" high, marked "SNA, Calif., USa," **$65.00 – 75.00.**

Pair of tan and black Siamese cats, 9" wide, 12" high, blue marble eyes, **$125.00 – 135.00.**

Pair of Siamese cats, topaz and tan blending; charcoal faces, tails, ears, and paws; 10" wide, 12" high, **$150.00 – 175.00.**

Snow white cats in a tan basket, 9" wide, 8½" high, **$150.00 – 165.00.**

Siamese mother cat with kitten, marked "Kron of Texas," 9" wide, 13" high, **$125.00 – 150.00.**

Side view of stylized smart cat, dripping shiny black glaze; sunset, tan, moss green, and turquoise; Canadian manufacturer, backlighted, 5" wide, 17½" high, $200.00 – 250.00.

Front view of previous cat.

Archival mist pair of Siamese reclining cats, spotted color, blue jeweled eyes, signed "Lane & Co., Van Nuys, Ca.," 13" wide, 13" high, $100.00 – 125.00.

Glossy pair of archival mist Siamese cats, curled tails, blue jeweled eyes, dark ash airbrushing, signed "LANE & CO. VAN NUYS, CALIF. © U.S.A.," 12" wide, 12" high, $100.00 – 125.00.

Very desirable black and white comedy and tragedy masks, circa 1950s, signed "Hedi Schoop," **$290.00 – 300.00.**

Very beautiful arched and agile ballet dancer, 9½" wide, circa 1952, **$100.00 – 110.00.**

Black and white musicians, 12" wide, circa 1950s, **$80.00 – 90.00.**

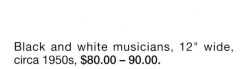

Bronzed ballerina with a swan, 12" wide, signed "Lane and Co.," $125.00 – 135.00.

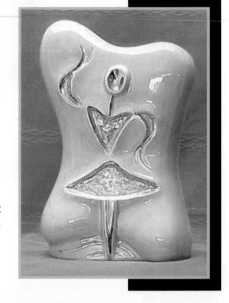

Gold ballet dancer, silhouetted against three-dimensional background, 7" wide, $75.00 – 85.00.

Mottled green and cream Royal Haeger comedy and tragedy mask, signed "Royal Haeger," 10" wide, $80.00 – 95.00.

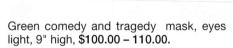

Green comedy and tragedy mask, eyes light, 9" high, $100.00 – 110.00.

Fancy detachable airbrushed dancers on a brass base, dark lettuce green front dish, upward lighting within the brass holder, 11½" wide, 12" high, **$150.00 – 160.00.**

Greenish-yellow Spanish dancers, 12" wide, 15" high, signed "Maddux 8008," **$80.00 – 90.00.**

Cloudy white Spanish dancers, 12" wide, 15" high, signed "Maddux," **$80.00 – 90.00.**

Glossy black nun, 6½" wide, 11" high, **$55.00 – 65.00.**

Ballerina dancer, ceramic, 5" wide, 8½" high, $55.00 – 65.00.

Cute airbrushed pair of lustered pink and gray dancers, 6½" wide, 9" high, $100.00 – 110.00.

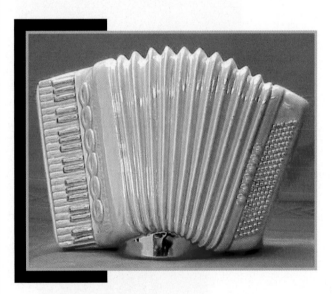

Pink accordion, accented in gold, 10" wide, $290.00 – 310.00.

Rare white accordion, gold tints, marked "Lawrence Welk," 10" wide, $485.00 – 500.00.

Dance, Music & Theatre

Pair of light tan Kron dancers on a drum, ceramic, with all original packaging, 9½" wide, 14" high, **$125.00 – 135.00.**

Flowing dancer with cornflower gown, 11" wide, 9" high, marked "Holland Mold," **$100.00 – 125.00.**

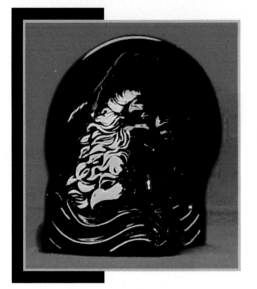

Mysterious glossy coal black lady wearing a wide brimmed hat, 9" wide, 9½" high, **$80.00 – 90.00.**

Shiny black and spattered gold Egyptian dancers, 12" wide, 11" high, **$100.00 – 125.00.**

Pair of chocolate African dancers garbed in white and yellow, brass screening, fiberglass shield, spinach green front dish, 15" wide, 12" high, **$150.00 – 165.00.**

Male and female ballerina dancers, Royal Haeger, pearl drippings, 11" wide, 10" high, **$85.00 – 100.00.**

Close-ups of the dancers.

Fancy pair of dancers painted and airbrushed in black, pink, green, and flesh tones; both are removable and mounted on a geometric brass base with removable ivy green planter/candy tray. Half oval light green fiberglass shield, lighted internally, central light encased in geometric brass, 11½" wide, 12" high, **$140.00 – 150.00.**

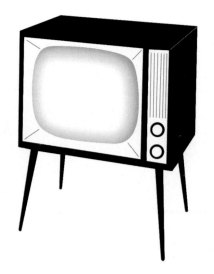

Sky blue double deer, 9" wide, circa 1950s, "Gilner," **$100.00 – 110.00.**

Light aqua 1950s reindeer, ceramic, 12" wide, 10½" high, **$125.00 – 135.00.**

Green and gold resting deer, 16" wide, 10½" high, **$125.00 – 135.00.**

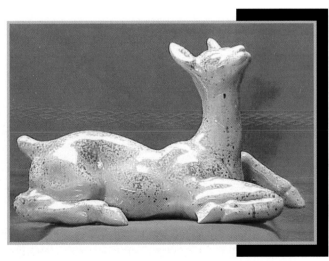

Airbrushed white deer with fawn, yellow and black highlights, 13½" wide, 10½" high, $100.00 – 125.00.

Maddux baby deer, lightly airbrushed, black highlights, 6½" wide, 6¼" high, signed "Maddux of Calif.," $45.00 – 55.00.

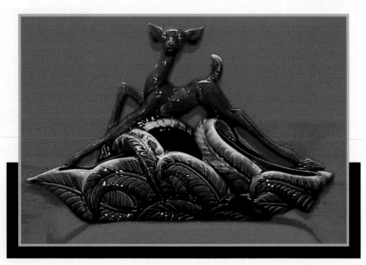

Tobacco-hued deer planter and TV light, 16" wide, 10" high, $45.00 – 55.00.

Snow white deer against a burgundy background, 7" wide, 8" high, **$40.00 – 50.00.**

Brown deer silhouetted against a creamy white ground, 11" wide, 9½" high, **$50.00 – 65.00.**

Airbrushed running double deer, 11" wide, 11" high, marked "Maddux of Calif. 1959," **$90.00 – 100.00.**

Airbrushed alert 1959 Lane deer, 13" wide, 12½" high, **$85.00 – 95.00.**

Bronze double deer, ceramic, circa 1950s, 11½" wide, 13" high, **$55.00 – 65.00.**

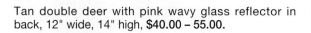

Tan double deer with pink wavy glass reflector in back, 12" wide, 14" high, **$40.00 – 55.00.**

Three blue-gray running deer, 11½" wide, 12½" high, **$50.00 – 65.00.**

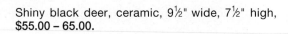

Shiny black deer, ceramic, 9½" wide, 7½" high, **$55.00 – 65.00.**

Light tan running deer, 10" wide, 5" high, **$45.00 – 60.00.**

Light tan double deer, signed "Kron," 7" wide, 15½" high, **$55.00 – 65.00.**

Nutmeg and white fawn with black spots, air-brushed, front dish, 10" wide, 12" high, **$85.00 – 100.00.** Shown with fruit in the dish.

Previous deer, shown without the fruit.

Taupe leaping deer, woodland base, backlighted, 13" wide, 12" high, **$85.00 – 100.00.**

Marbleized and stylized leaping deer, green, backlighted, 15" wide, 10" high, $85.00 – 100.00.

Antique tan double deer, back planter, backlighted, 11" wide, 9½" high, $85.00 – 100.00.

Halo effect 3-D silhouetted running deer, airbrushed fawn, moss and black land base, signed "Maddux of Calif. Made in U.S.A.," 10" wide, 10" high, $75.00 – 85.00.

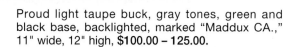

Proud light taupe buck, gray tones, green and black base, backlighted, marked "Maddux CA.," 11" wide, 12" high, $100.00 – 125.00.

Plaster-of-Paris Art Deco dying stag, creamy marble with gold and black tips, backlighted, 17" wide, 14" high, **$125.00 – 150.00.**

Bronze doe and fawn on a base, backlighted, unmarked Haeger, 12" wide, 12" high, **$150.00 – 175.00.**

Mauve-gray running doe and fawn on a wooden base; multicolored green, black, and nutmeg; back planter and light, marked "Maddux Cal. © 1959," 11½" wide, 11½" high, **$175.00 – 200.00.**

Sunny yellow fawn on Art Deco green base, two pressed glass flowers in pink and green, 6½" diameter, 12" high, **$70.00 – 80.00.**

Glazed light brown running deer against a leafy base, dual planter, backlighted, 10" wide, 4" high, **$45.00 – 60.00.**

COLORS

The reader is encouraged to note the color(s) associated with each lamp by viewing photos and visualizing the color(s) named. Names assigned on the Crescent Matboard color chart are provided, as are colors associated with foods and nature.

CRESCENT MATBOARD COLORS

Persimmon, Red Brite Cores, Really Red, Chinese Red, Crimson, Cranberry, Purple Purple, Sunset Clay, Oriental Red, True Red, Cerise, Azalea, Madeira Red, Las Cruces Purple, Pottery, Hibiscus, Heather, Taos, Venetian Red, Red, Cherub Pink, Light Mauve, Wine, Violet, Madagascar Pink, Heather Mist, Garnet, Majestic Purple, Peach Moire, Limoges Pink, Pink RagMoire, Rose Pink Marble, Burgundy Marble, Purple Wildflower, Candle Light, Cameo Rose, Pastel Pink, Ice Mauve, Deep Purple, Black Currant, Rouge, Rose, Taupe, Camelot, Sheraton Rose, Grey Violet, French Lilac, Airbrushed Copper, Santa Fe, Indian Red, Rose Gold, Rubia, Maroon, Periwinkle Blue, Redwood, Pompeian Red, Riviera Rose, Nutmeg, Mauve, Wineberry, Deep Lilac, Russet, Bricke, Classic Brown, Auburn, Burgundy Gold Marble, Burgundy Moire, Concord, Brick Red, Williamsburg Red, Hazelnut, Boulder Brown, Burgundy, Carmine, Amethyst, Off White, Oyster White, Light Gray Marble, Ivory, French Buff, White, Ivory Parchment, Cream, Eggshell, Off White/Cream, Smoked Pearl, White Rice Paper, Antique Gray, Bridal Veil, Spice Ivory, Cream, Dark Cream, Silver Gray, Antique White, White Moire, Cream Linen, Wheat, Alabaster, Winter White, Pompano Beach White, Searstone, Pearl RagMoire, Antique Lace, Off White Ribbed, Palm Beach White, Lily White, Warm White, Tan Rice Paper, Tan, Snow White, White and Cream, Ivory, Vintage Gray, Canvas White, White and Cream Pebble, White Linen, Antique Ivory, Archival Mist, Arctic White, Porcelain, Script White, Brite White, Manor White, Light Cream, Very White, Cream Rice Paper, English Cream, Antique Buff, Smooth Black, Expresso, Black Opal, Black, Raven Black, Antique Tan, Cream, English Cream, Antique Gray, Desert Sand, Olde Ecru, Neutral Gray, Rouge, Green Pear, Green Apple, Daffodil, Yellow Brite Cores, Naples Yellow, Topaz, Mandarin, Moss Point Green, Sheer Lime, Light Jonquil, Chamois Gold, Saffron, Burnt Orange, Moss, Laurel, Custard, Cognac, Sautern, Cream Marble, Tea Rose, Silver Leaf, Flaxen, Rust, Apricot, Sage, Oatmeal, Pewter, Peach, Doeskin, Raffia, Desert Sand, Grass Green, Sandstone, Saddle Tan, Suntan, Dusty Rose, Avocado, Dark Umbria, Sand, Green Gold Marble, Fossil, Oak Brown, Sepia, Dark Olive, Ochre, Sable, Black Walnut, Fudge, Ultramarine, China Blue, Blue Belle, Aruba, Malachite, Kelly Green, Patriot Blue, Sheer Blue, Marine Blue, Bimini Blue, Art Deco Green, Cornflower, Sky Blue, Persian Blue, Azure, Green Marble, Paris Green, Lupine, Twilight, Laurel Green, Soft Green, Light Blue Marble, French Blue, Volcano Blue, Imperial Blue, Tapestry, Blue Slate, Ocean Mist, Delft Blue, Lapis, Light Teal, Ivy Green, Indigo, Blue Marble, Deep Sea, Country Blue, Dusk, Williamsburg Green, Dark Blue, Light Blue, Storm Blue, Devonshire Blue, Alpine Green, Foxhunt Green, Navy, Newport Blue, Baltic Blue, Williamsburg Blue, Black Watch, Cobalt, Flanders Blue, Obsidian, Pyrite, French Gray, Olde Gray, Herringbone, Rose Gray, Gunmetal, Aged Bronze, Silver Black Marble, Stone Gray, English Stone, Rose Marble, Sea Gull, Pearl, Pewter, Dark Ash, Smoke Parchment, Silver Foil, Etched Silver, Autumn Mist, Regent Gray, Fog, Gray Rice Paper, Medium Gray, Sea Shell, Medium Gray Marble, Mist Gray, German Silver, Oxford, Dusty Blue, Dawn Gray, Ashen, Gray Plum, Gibraltar Gray, Copley Gray, Granite, Windsor Blue, Bar Harbor Gray, Medium Gold Florentine, Yellow Gold Florentine, Thin Gold Foil, 24 Karat, Champagne Gold, Spanish Gold, Pale Gold, Grecian Gold, Roman Bronze.

NATURALISTIC COLORS

Alabaster White, Snow White, Rice White, Marshmallow White, Fluffy Cloud White, Refrigerator White, Polar Bear White, Pearl White, Abalone Iridescent, Cotton Candy Pink, Watermelon Pink, Salmon Pink, Olive Black, Shiny Coal Black, Licorice Black, Lime Green, Kiwi Green, Spinach Green, Lettuce Green, Broccoli Green, Sage Green, Banana Green, Endive Green, Cabbage Green, Mallard Green, Apple Green, Olive Green, Pea Green, Banana Yellow, Lime Yellow, Lemon Yellow, Peach Yellow, Radish Red, Strawberry Red, Cherry Red, Raspberry Red, Tomato Red, Cranberry Red, Candy Cane Red, Hollyberry Red, Coffee Brown, Chocolate Brown, Date Brown, Honey Brown, Liquid Carmel, Violet Blue, Sky Blue, Turquoise Blue, Maroon, Chartreuse, Tangerine Orange, Cantaloupe Orange, Pumpkin Orange, Corn Husk Tan, Gourd Tan, Peanut, Brazil Nut, Chestnut, Almond, Plum, Apricot, Grape, Tree Bark, Lavender.

Brown and tan Maddux basset hound, 8" wide, 11½" high, all original packaging, **$145.00 – 160.00.**

Pair of black and tan boxers, 10" wide, marked "Claes 1954," **$125.00 – 135.00.**

Cautious little puppy, 9" wide, 5½" high, **$45.00 – 55.00.**

Begging poodle, 4½" wide, 12½" high, ceramic, **$70.00 – 85.00.**

D O G S

Green dog with a basket, 9" wide, 8" high, $55.00 – 65.00.

Colorful airbrushed hunting dog, 14" wide, 9" high, $100.00 – 125.00.

Four ceramic puppies in a box, 9" wide, $190.00 – 200.00.

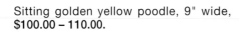

Sitting golden yellow poodle, 9" wide, $100.00 – 110.00.

Poised pink poodle, ceramic, 7" wide, $100.00 – 115.00.

Frolicsome white poodle, 8" wide, 11½" high, $55.00 – 65.00.

Running black greyhound, 12" wide, 8" high, $55.00 – 65.00.

Brown dachshund, circa 1950s, 15" wide, 8" high, $100.00 – 110.00.

Glistening gold-glazed Scottie, 12" wide, 9" high, $85.00 – 95.00.

Blue-gray greyhound, 12" wide, 8" high, 1950s, ceramic, $65.00 – 75.00.

Pink and gray fancy poodles, ceramic, with planter, marked "Lane & Co.," all original packaging, $100.00 – 125.00.

Airbrushed poodle and lady head vase, ceramic, 9" wide, circa 1950s, came with original box, packaging, and instructions, $290.00 – 300.00.

Pair of shiny coal black Afghan hounds, 10½" wide, 13" high, **$85.00 – 95.00.**

Ceramic spinach green dog, 4" wide, 7½" high, **$65.00 – 75.00.**

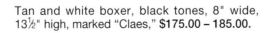

Yellow and white sitting collie, 9½" wide, 11½" high, **$110.00 – 125.00.**

Tan and white boxer, black tones, 8" wide, 13½" high, marked "Claes," **$175.00 – 185.00.**

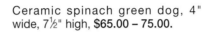

Begging dachshund, brown with black accents, 7" wide, 13½" high, **$150.00 – 165.00.**

Pair of sitting classic brown spaniels, 9" wide, 9" high, **$100.00 – 125.00.**

Mottled black and white pointer with pheasant in his mouth, 10" wide, 8" high, **$100.00 – 125.00.**

English cocker spaniel, contrasting black and white, 6½" wide, 11" high, **$150.00 – 175.00.**

Bronzed dog sitting erect, 9" wide, 11½" high, **$135.00 – 150.00.**

Scottie pulling a wagon; shades of tan, black, green, and madeira red; central glass flower lights, pressed glass leaves and flowers in hues of pink, blue, green, and yellow; 5½" wide, 12" high, **$65.00 – 75.00.**

Joined white poodle and nutmeg pug, amber eyes that light up, marked "KRON ® Texans Inc. Bangs, Texas," 12" wide, 13" high, **$75.00 – 95.00.**

Tan-bodied double spaniels, nutmeg trim, signed "CLAES COPYRIGHT © 56," eyes light, backlighted, 12" wide, 9" high, **$120.00 – 135.00.**

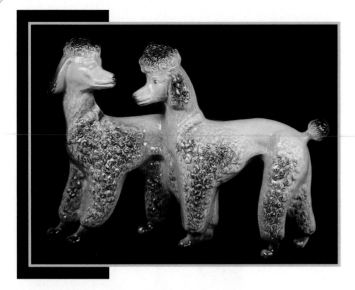

Pink and silver-gray double poodles, 14" wide, 10" high, marked "Lane & Co. LA. CAL. © 1956," **$85.00 – 100.00.**

Nutmeg double greyhounds, lime green drippings, designed by Royal Hickman at Haeger, backlighted, back planter, 11" wide, 13" high, **$175.00 – 200.00.**

Molded and airbrushed plaster-of-Paris German shepherd on rock base, tapered lime green conical fiberglass shade; lemon yellow, black, and tan hues; 12" wide, 11" high, signed "METRO ART ©," **$90.00 – 115.00.**

Handsome and heavy apple green plaster-of-Paris hearth, two flower/candleholders, green fiberglass shield with an arch, airbrushed sandstone and black German shepherd, original red plastic collar, signed "Sculpture Ware," 14" wide, 9" high, **$135.00 – 150.00.**

Single glazed and detailed ocean mist flower with leaves, 7" wide, 9½" high, **$50.00 – 60.00.**

Single glazed and detailed wine-hued flower with leaves, 7" wide, 9½" high, **$50.00 – 60.00.**

Glazed appliance white two-petal flower, green and gold trim, 8½" wide, 9" high, **$45.00 – 55.00.**

Dark ivy green glazed shell on a base, 7" wide, 10" high, $45.00 – 55.00.

Three glazed green corner trees, white rail fencing, green grass, 8" wide, 6" high, $55.00 – 65.00.

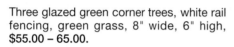

Paris green serrated leaf, powdered gold hints, 9½" wide, 11½" high, $55.00 – 65.00.

Glossy blue-gray vines, 11" wide, 6" high, $50.00 – 60.00.

Satin leather brown three-leaf clover, 9½" wide, 9" high, signed "Treasure Craft," **$40.00 – 50.00.**

Shiny bluish-white leaf with golden highlights, 10½" wide, 8½" high, **$50.00 – 60.00.**

Pair of airbrushed light and dark brown leaves, 8½" wide, 9½" high, **$55.00 – 65.00.**

Glossy tan and white airbrushed flower, black base, 7" wide, 12½" high, **$45.00 – 55.00.**

Round white light with leaves painted green, gold, and cranberry, 6½" wide, 10" high, **$45.00 – 55.00.**

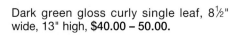

Dark green gloss curly single leaf, 8½" wide, 13" high, **$40.00 – 50.00.**

Chartreuse and cream flower vase on a black base, 7" wide, 11½" high, **$50.00 – 60.00.**

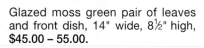

Glazed moss green pair of leaves and front dish, 14" wide, 8½" high, **$45.00 – 55.00.**

Glazed multihued brown and white three-leaf vase, 9" wide, 12" high, $40.00 – 50.00.

Green iridescent malachite leaf, with planter, light yellow and dark green drippings, 9½" diameter, 7½" high, $50.00 – 65.00.

Ivory parchment basketweave cornucopia shell vase, gold trim at the top and base, icy mauve rose and buds, sage leaves, 8½" wide, 11½" high, marked "4730" on the base, $85.00 – 100.00.

Close-up of the flowers.

Spinach green scalloped leaf on a scrolled base, lights internally, 6" wide, 9" high, **$75.00 – 95.00.**

Four-petal green briar vase-type light, black Oriental base, lights internally and shows through slits in the leaves, 7" wide, 12" high, **$100.00 – 125.00.**

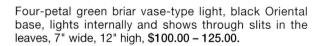

Circa 1920s purple, orange, green, and blue bronzed peacock on a white onyx footed base, four bulbs in the back, stamped "Made in France," cut and faceted, 11 jeweled panels of beads, 16" wide, 25" high, **$2,500.00 – 3,000.00.**

Gilded cranberry and archival mist flower lamp, internal bulb, 8½" wide, 9" high, **$75.00 – 95.00.**

Multicolored bronze gilded peacock, 11 jeweled panels, rust-hued onyx footed base, three light sockets in the back, marked "Made in France," 16" wide, 25" high, **$2,500.00 – 3,000.00.**

Pair of small brass gilded peacocks with colorful glass beaded tails, 8" wide, 12" high, **$1,500.00 – 1,700.00 each.**

Close-up of one peacock lamp.

Close-up of the back of the same lamp detailing woven wires that hold the glass beads in place.

Close-up of peacock's face and gilding.

Another close-up, showing additional detailing.

Art Deco millefiori (glass of "a thousand flowers") lamp on a rectangular black marble base having gold veining, bronze dancer with carved ivory face, 9" wide, 9" high, **$1,500.00 – 2,000.00.**

Magnificent pair of crystal Fostoria seahorses, pressed crystal plumes above, gilded metal two-socket base, 9" wide, 15" high, **$800.00 – 1,000.00.**

Gilded metal fruit basket with animal feet and ornate ram-head handles, central raised jeweled medallion, filled with multi-hued glass fruit, 15" wide, 7" high, **$2,500.00 – 3,000.00.**

Monumental and rare array of multicolored glass flowers in orange, blue, pink, and lime green. Secured with plaster in a Roseville container measuring 9½" wide and 6½" high. The copper wires are wound with fine silk thread, which often frays and makes the lamp almost impossible to rewire. Overall width, 14", 29" high, **$1,500.00 – 2,000.00.**

Close-ups showing detailing of the flowers.

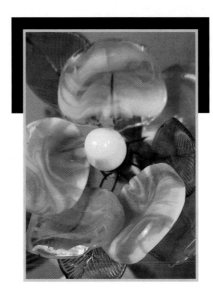

Flared lead crystal glass basket, glass pedestal insert holds silk-wrapped multicolored flowers in place, 15" wide, 10" high, **$250.00 – 275.00.**

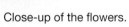

Close-up of the flowers.

Czechoslovakian cut-glass beaded basket and handles, strung on metal wires, colorful glass fruit in the basket, from the 1930s, 13" from handle to handle, 7½" high, **$2,500.00 – 3,000.00.**

Close-up of the realistic fruit.

Close-up of the medallion on the basket.

Art Nouveau pewter-finish fruit basket, Czechoslovakian, light in the basket, fruit all wired together, mirrored wooden base, 13½" from handle to handle, 6" wide, **$2,500.00 – 3,000.00.**

Close-up showing the intricate backing of the wired fruit.

Czechoslovakian peasant girl carrying glass poppies, each basket lights, pewter with an antique finish, 8" wide, 13½" high, **$1,000.00 – 1,500.00.**

Czechoslovakian low-footed glass compote, pumpkin orange spattered with red and yellow, multicolored fruit in the bowl, lights up, 8½" wide, 8½" high, **$2,500.00 – 3,000.00.**

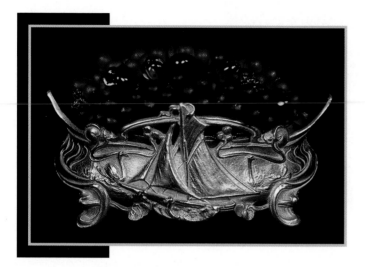

Gilded ornate pewter basket with glass fruit, Czechoslovakian, basket has unusual animal feet and ram-head handles, 15" wide, 7" high, **$2,500.00 – 3,000.00.**

Cherub pink youngsters holding hands, pressed glass flowers in variegated pink, yellow, blue, and apricot, 3½" diameter, 15" high, **$70.00 – 80.00.**

Close-up of children.

Backlighted ivy green scalloped and gilded cabbage leaves, two front planters, 12" wide, 7" high, signed "CALIF.," **$80.00 – 100.00.**

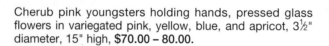

COLLECTING TV LAMPS

- We live to collect the past.
- People collect what they like, for fun and profit.
- The nostalgic era associated with TV lamps has made them items worth looking for, admiring, and purchasing.
- Prices for perfect working examples presently range from $10 to $300.
- TV lamps are an important part of the news media development.
- These early lamps created both indirect lighting and a decorative atmosphere.
- Placed on top of the TV, these attractive lamps helped one avoid eyestrain and also made for pleasant conversation.
- A lamp served as a focal point in any room, and a color combination could be built around it.
- Lamps also served as planters for live and artificial flowers/leaves.
- Some lamps had one or more pockets that could be used to hold coins, candy, jewelry, and the like. Others also incorporated clocks.
- Television lamps are avidly sought and appreciated by all ages, but especially Baby Boomers, those enjoying middle and retirement age.
- TV lamps are pieces of art; they are sturdy, pleasing to the eye, and have clean, flowing lines.
- Some examples are extremely realistic; figures not only look muscular, but as if they are capable of graceful and sensual movement.
- A list of known manufacturers has been provided. Sparse information is available concerning the companies. Some lamps were impressed with logos, while others carried only paper labels. Many labels have been lost over the years.
- Correct wattage for bulbs in all lamps would be between 25 and 40 watts. In some instances, torpedo bulbs fit better than regular bulbs.
- Some lamps possess portholes that provide additional attractive lighting.
- Crossover collecting is possible with TV lamps. A bird lamp, for example, might appeal not only to a lamp collector, but also to a bird enthusiast.
- Enjoy the lamps that you collect; use them often. Check the wiring, and always replace it when necessary to avoid fire, smoke damage, or even scorching. Rewiring does not reduce the value of a lamp.
- Do not be surprised to see planters, in various colors and by competing vendors, in the same styles as TV lamps.
- All types of models and styles were created by lamp manufacturers.
- TV lamps were extremely popular in the 1950s.
- As technology and cabinet designs improved, TV lamps were discarded to closets or attics.
- Now there is a rebirth and revival of TV lamps, as they are shown at auctions, flea markets, cooperatives, and antique shops.
- Prices vary as one travels north, south, east, and west throughout the U.S.
- Add 30% to a lamp with an original shade in excellent condition.
- Do not purchase lamps that are badly crazed or chipped.
- Lamps that are overpriced should be rejected.
- Perhaps TV lamps have descended from Art Deco radio lamps popular in the 1920s and 1930s.
- Other lamps may have evolved from the 1930s-style torchieres, which provided upward lighting. These were constructed from brass, plastics, and imitation bamboo.
- While doing my research for this book, I discovered numerous reproduction lamps and TV lamp types, both on the Internet and in antique cooperatives. Collectors should study the examples shown, noting shapes, measurements, details, and colors. New pieces will not show scratches, chips, honest wear, crazing in the glaze, worn fixtures and cords, etc.

Airbrushed Conestoga wagon, 9" wide, 6" high, **$65.00 – 75.00.**

Lively airbrushed Native American with bow and arrow and chasing a deer, 9" wide, **$100.00 – 110.00.**

Ceramic covered wagon, tan and brown shading, **$50.00 – 60.00.**

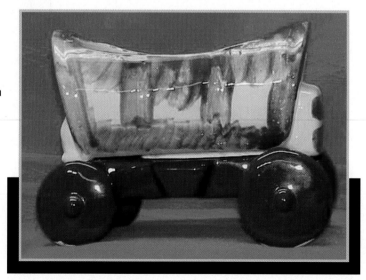

Buffalo, various brown shades, 12" wide, $150.00 – 165.00.

Green coach with wire wheels, lights internally, 10" wide, $75.00 – 85.00.

Black Conestoga wagon with golden hints, 8½" wide, 10" high, $65.00 – 75.00.

Airbrushed horse and covered wagon, 10" wide, with original packaging, marked "Rolso 1-164 53/302," $55.00 – 65.00.

Dark green stagecoach with golden highlights, 9" wide, 6" high, $55.00 – 65.00.

Washington, Lincoln, Jefferson, and Roosevelt (Theodore) on Mount Rushmore, chalk white, 9" wide, 10" high, signed "Maddux of Calif.," $165.00 – 185.00.

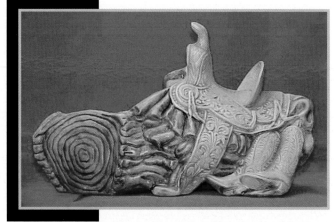

Creamy yellow cowboy boots and saddle on a log, 13" wide, 7" high, signed "Maddux of Calif. 1960 E-21855-M," $100.00 – 125.00.

Topaz wagon wheel on Art Deco green grass, 12" wide, 13" high, $125.00 – 135.00.

Shiny coal black stagecoach, trimmed in gold, top planter, backlighted, 8½" wide, 5¼" high, **$45.00 – 60.00.**

Reproduction plaster-of-Paris wise Native American storyteller and his son, swirls of smoke reveal a hunter on horseback after three bison, eagle and wolf, lights internally, light shows through 15 slits, painted in multicolored hues, colored with sparkles, signed "S B," 7½" wide, 11" high, **$30.00 – 40.00.**

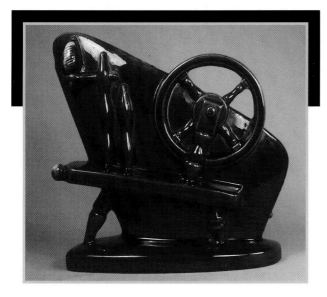

Glossy detailed tobacco brown spinning wheel, four turned spokes, minor white highlights, backlighted, 8½" wide, 10½" high, **$55.00 – 65.00.**

Close-up of spinning wheel.

TELEVISION LAMP MANUFACTURERS

- Hedi Schoop Creations, North Hollywood, California (mid-1950s)
- Alden Hollywood Productions
- Hollywood Eran
- Wayne of Hollywood
- Hollywood Ceramics
- Hollywood Creation
- California Originals, Torrence, California
- Miramar of California (1950s)
- Treasure Craft, Compton, California
- Norfleet of California
- Made in California, U.S.A.
- Cali-Co of California
- Enchanto of California
- Royal Fleet of California
- La Velle of California
- Marcia of California, Los Angeles
- Sawage of California
- Le Ann of California
- Ceramic Arts of California
- SNAS of California
- Zill Hutchins of California
- Lanell of California
- Sierra-Columbia of Pasadena, California, and Los Angeles, California
- Alert Lamp Company of Los Angeles, California
- Easher Company of Los Angeles, California
- Gidget Fair Stores of San Francisco, California
- Genie Ceramics of Lynwood, California
- Modernera Lamp of Los Angeles, California
- Maddux of California, Los Angeles, California (1937 – 1974)
- Lane and Co. of Van Nuys, California (1956 – 1966)
- Royal Haeger, California and also Dundee and Macomb, Illinois
- American Art Potteries, Morton, Illinois, paper labels (1947 – 1963)

- Premco Mfg. Co., Chicago, Illinois
- Navis and Smith Co., Chicago, Illinois
- Gonder Ceramic Arts, Inc., Zanesville, Ohio
- Fuhry and Sons, Cleveland, Ohio
- Royal China and Novelty Company, Sebring, Ohio
- Phil-Mar Corporation, Cleveland, Ohio
- Midwest Potteries, Inc. (1940 – 1944)
- G. I. Trevino
- Duncan (1954)
- Florence Art
- Sierra Columbia, Pasadena, California
- McCoy, Roseville, Ohio
- Van Briggle Pottery, Colorado Springs, Colorado
- Kron (designer) of Bangs, Texas. Worked for Texans, Inc. Some known designs are TV lamps featuring pugs, poodles, Siamese cats, and an owl.
- American China
- Schor-Par Craft of New York
- Gilner Co.
- C. Miller Co.
- Kleine Co.
- Dixon Art Studios
- Italy
- Japan
- Holland
- Rosemeade (Wahpeton Pottery Co.)
- CSM (1935)
- Rock-O-Stone
- La Miane China
- Williams China
- Sheridan China
- Buckingham Ceramics
- Puccini Novelty Art Co.
- American Statuary
- PGH Statuary
- Waico TV Lamps
- Stnola Lamps

- Luminart
- Made by Donna
- Garland Creations
- Comer Creation
- Hallfield
- L.M. Fielack (artist) for Metro Art
- "A Criterion Product, Japan"
- Williams Ceramics (Claes Copyright U.S.A./Designer)
- "Lampcraft American China, 22 karat Gold, Hand Decorated" in raised letters, on a gold foil label with red background
- Zini Pat.
- L. Pellegrini & Co.
- Modern Art Products, Kansas City, Missouri
- Bilt-Rite Mfg. Co., Chicago, Illinois
- Metro Ware
- Esgo-Light Corporation
- Duquesne Statuary
- Silvestri Brothers
- "Crenshaw No. C-401"
- Esco-Lite
- Northington
- Stewart B. McCullough
- Helmscene, Grand Rapids, Michigan
- Tri-Wonder Lamp, Madison, Wisconsin
- H. L. Green Co. Inc.
- "Limi Nov 306"
- Walsco JVL Miramar, California
- Esco-Lite Co., Los Angeles, California
- Enconolite
- Bircraft
- Camark
- "Hand Decorated in California, BELL CERAMICS, INC."
- Beauceware
- Lawrin Co., Chicago
- "© Columbia Statuary"
- Relic Art Ltd., Brooklyn, New York ("Relic Art")

Light tan horse with saddle, ceramic, 1951, 9½" wide, $100.00 – 110.00.

Black and white horse heads, 9½" wide, 11½" high, $140.00 – 150.00.

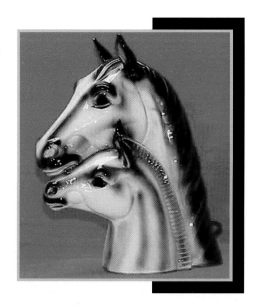

Boulder brown horse in front of rustic fencing, air-brushed, 9½" wide, 11" high, $85.00 – 95.00.

Light tan Art Deco horse head, 11" wide, 9½" high, $65.00 – 70.00.

Hazelnut horse head with colt, 9" wide, 8" high, $75.00 – 85.00.

Striking red flambé running horse against black ground, white highlights, 10" wide, 7" high, $55.00 – 65.00.

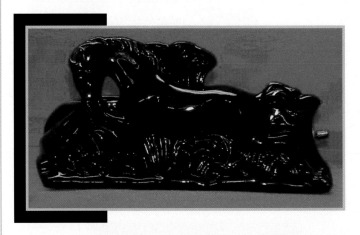

Black horse, 1950s, 10½" wide, 5¼" high, $75.00 – 85.00.

Light tan double horse heads, double planters, 9½" wide, 5" high, $50.00 – 60.00.

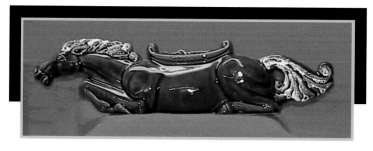

Elongated and dark-glazed nutmeg brown horse, 20" wide, 5" high, signed "C. Miller USA.," $75.00 – 85.00.

Gray horse head, ceramic, 9½" wide, 14" high, $85.00 – 95.00.

Airbrushed Lane and Company ceramic horse; tan, black, white, and green; 11" wide, 13" high, $95.00 – 110.00.

Marvelous marshmallow white circus horse with gold trim, 10" wide, 14" high, $110.00 – 125.00.

Black ceramic horse head, circa 1950s, 8" wide, 14½" high, **$80.00 – 90.00.**

Wonderful glossy black and white running horse, ceramic, circa 1950s, 13½" wide, 12" high, signed "Lane and Co. Van Nuys, Calif.," **$90.00 – 110.00.**

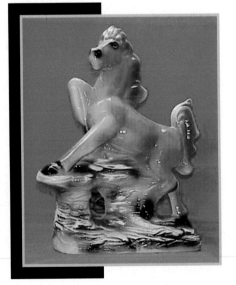

Airbrushed saffron prancing horse on rock, 11" wide, 14" high, **$70.00 – 85.00.**

A comparison of the preceding horse. Airbrushed saffron stallion on black and white cliff, with the addition of an attacking black panther, marked "Kron 1958," **$160.00 – 175.00.**

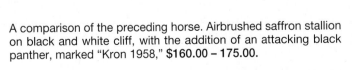

Tall and proud green and gold rearing horse, 11" wide, 13" high, **$55.00 – 70.00.**

Light mauve rearing horses, highlighted white manes, 11" wide, 13" high, **$75.00 – 85.00.**

Draped bright yellow horse, 12" wide, 12" high, fully signed "Lane and Co. Van Nuys, Calif. #8524," **$90.00 – 110.00.**

Malachite green double jumping horses, 11½" wide, 10½" high, **$80.00 – 95.00.**

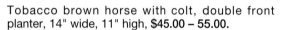

Light tan horse head, light inside the green reflector wreath, 11½" wide, 8½" long, **$110.00 – 125.00.**

Tobacco brown horse with colt, double front planter, 14" wide, 11" high, **$45.00 – 55.00.**

Yellow green jumping horse on dark green ground, 13" wide, 10" high, **$45.00 – 55.00.**

Banana yellow jumping ceramic horse, 11½" wide, 9" high, **$40.00 – 55.00.**

Unusual two-tone purple marble-like horse head, 7" wide, 10½" high, **$80.00 – 90.00.**

Moss green running horse, 13" wide, 11" high, **$80.00 – 90.00.**

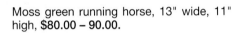

Horse head, midnight green with hints of blue, 8" wide, 10" high, **$65.00 – 75.00.**

Stylized apple green horse, 12" wide, 10" high, signed "Gilner," **$45.00 – 55.00.**

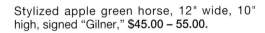

Nicely styled green and gold horse head, highlighted with 22-karat gold, 9½" wide, 9" high, signed "Beachcombers, Calif. Genuine Porcelain," **$80.00 – 95.00.** (Most TV lamps with gold application were decorated with 22-karat gold).

Airbrushed gray racehorses and jockeys on a white background, 9½" wide, 9½" high, **$80.00 – 95.00.**

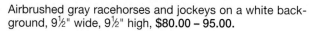

Pair of proud light brown horse heads, 13" wide, 8½" high, **$55.00 – 65.00.**

Light green horse head silhouetted within a horseshoe, 7" wide, 9" high, **$40.00 – 50.00.**

Black walnut brown arched-legs horse, green fiberglass screen in the back, 11" wide, 10½" high, $85.00 – 90.00.

Apple green donkey with cart, 11" wide, 10" high, $40.00 – 55.00.

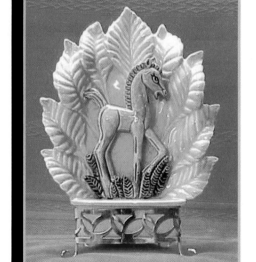

Light green and gold horse, brass base, 8" wide, 11" high, signed "Miramar of Calif. 1956-608," $80.00 – 95.00.

Fancy arched tobacco-hued horse, green slag glass shield, 11" wide, 10½" high, $85.00 – 95.00.

Prancing white horse on a black background, 11" wide, 9" high, **$75.00 – 85.00.**

Two light yellow rearing horses highlighted with gold, 9" wide, 7½" high, **$75.00 – 95.00.**

Mustard yellow pony in front of a fence, 8" wide, 11½" high, **$55.00 – 65.00.**

Prancing burgundy horse silhouetted against a rayed background, 6½" wide, 8½" high, **$40.00 – 50.00.**

Light jonquil prancing horse among tall vegetation, 9½" wide, 9½" high, **$40.00 – 50.00.**

Caramel brown ceramic horse on a swirled base, 10½" wide, 11" high, **$35.00 – 45.00.**

Ceramic brown horse head, nicely silhouetted within a horseshoe, 9" wide, 6" high, **$25.00 – 35.00.**

Brown shaded galloping horse with wild mane and tail, on a light violet gilded base, 15" wide, 11" high, **$100.00 – 120.00.**

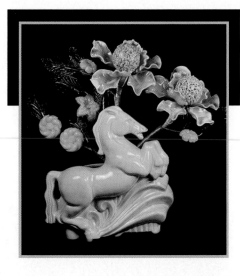

Chartreuse prancing horse, glass flowers set in plaster in the planter, two flowers with lights, 14" wide, 14" high, $65.00 – 85.00.

Ebony reclining horse, gray drippings; multicolored yellow, orange, and cobalt blue glass flowers; 14" wide, 14" high, $125.00 – 150.00.

Stylized licorice black horse on leather-hued base, backlighted, back planter, 15" wide, 13" high, $100.00 – 125.00.

Classic brown prancing horse, triple-back planter, backlighted, lime green drippings, 15" wide, 11" high, $85.00 – 95.00.

Ebony galloping horse, white and gray highlights, front dish, signed "Lane & Co. Van Nuys CA © 1957," 15½" wide, 14" high, **$150.00 – 175.00**.

Caramel jumping horse, brown woodland base, back planter and light, 14" wide, 10" high, **$65.00 – 85.00**.

Glossy hazelnut running mare and colt, creamy yellow manes and tails, backlighting, 10" wide, 9" high, **$50.00 – 60.00**.

Nutmeg mother horse with baby colt, lime green and tan drippings, double front planter, backlighted, 14" wide, 11" high, **$85.00 – 100.00**.

Classic brown and tan running horse and colt among grasses, tinge of lime green, 10" wide, 8¼" high, **$85.00 – 100.00.**

Bright white prancing stallion against rocky crags, backlighted, 10¼" wide, 12" high, **$75.00 – 90.00.**

Glazed taupe prancing stallion, airbrushed in raven black and moss green, backlighted, 10½" wide, 13" high, signed "Lane & Co. Van Nuys, Calif © 1958 – #L — 18," **$95.00 – 110.00.**

Unusual three-piece set, glossy licorice black with gold trim, lamp shown without the shade, 5" wide, 14½" high, three-way switch for lamps and TV light, pair of planters shaped like horse's hooves, 4¼" wide, 3" high, **$120.00 – 135.00 set.**

Land moss airbrushed proud horse, fawn-colored mane and tail, backlighted, 12" wide, 14" high, signed "Lane — Van Nuys CA © 1958," **$85.00 – 95.00.**

Parks' first TV lamp — Palomino colored prancing horse, multicolored base, white mane, tail, and chest, signed "Maddux Cal.," backlighted, 12" wide, 12½" high, priceless to them! **$125.00 – 150.00.**

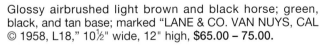

Small earth-toned prancing horse, front dish fawn color, horse's mane and tail are black, signed "Lane & Co. Van Nuys Cal © 1959," 10" wide, 12" high, **$95.00 – 110.00.**

Glossy airbrushed light brown and black horse; green, black, and tan base; marked "LANE & CO. VAN NUYS, CAL © 1958, L18," 10½" wide, 12" high, **$65.00 – 75.00.**

Proud prancing horse, fawn shaded, black mane and tail, tan front candy dish, green base, airbrushed finish, marked "Van Nuys CA © 1959," 14" wide, 13" high, **$125.00 – 150.00.**

Nutmeg shaded prancing horse, black mane and tail, white chest, boots, and nose markings, moss and tan base, backlighted, marked "Maddux of Ca.," 12" wide, 12½" high, **$125.00 – 150.00.**

Black horse and colt, marbled mane and tail, base is a grass formation, backlighted, 11" wide, 9" high, **$65.00 – 75.00.**

Madeira red chess horse head, backlighted, 10" long, 14" high, **$100.00 – 125.00.**

Nutmeg-colored horse head chess piece, back-lighted, 7" wide, 14½" high, $80.00 – 90.00.

Satin charcoal black chess horse on a natural wooden base, bronze mane, signed with Haeger paper label, backlighted, 9" wide, 12½" high, **$100.00 – 120.00**.

Shiny coal black intertwined stallions,12" wide, 10" high, **$85.00 – 100.00**.

Chartreuse double racing horses, green and blue base, original Royal Haeger paper label, backlighted, back planter, 18" wide, 11" high. **$100.00 – 120.00**.

Close-up of original paper label.

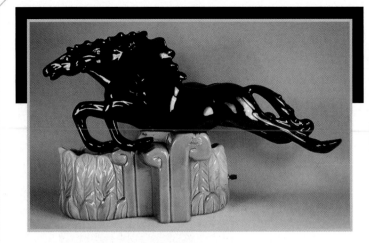

Shiny black double racing horses, chartreuse decorative base, back planter and light, 18" wide, 11" high, $200.00 – 225.00.

Art Deco arched-neck stallion, stylized mane and tail, feathered hooves; jet black with hues of green, purple, and gray; 18" wide, 17½" high, rear planter, backlighted, $250.00 – 300.00.

Art Deco stallion with original Haeger paper label which reads "Caution to avoid damage and overheating use finger bulb only!" $275.00 – 325.00.

Iridescent malachite double horse heads, blue-green manes, front double planter, backlighted, foil label reads "Haeger," 14" wide, 11" high, frontal view, $100.00 – 120.00.

Back view of the same horses.

Malachite green prancing horse, blue-green tail and mane, backlighted, back planter, gold foil label reads "Haeger," 14" wide, 11½" high, **$150.00 – 175.00.**

Mustard yellow rearing horse planter and TV light, original paper label, "TOMEONI — E 21926," 11 " wide, 10½" high, **$70.00 – 85.00.**

Shiny airbrushed muscular coal black jumping horse with chalky white overglaze above lettuce green leaves and rocks, backlighted, 12½" wide, 10" high, **$45.00 – 55.00.**

DESIGNING WITH TV LAMPS

Beautiful, colorful, and varied TV lamps from the 1950s proved to be unique conversation pieces in the home. People purchased lamps not only to light the areas around their televisions, but to also create individual identities that would be reflected within their living rooms.

Lamps are admired again today as they were when new. They have the ability to energize any area of the home and create a distinctive setting. These lamps have aged gracefully. They will become even more valuable as supply spirals downward.

- A person with a green thumb may wish to choose one or several lamps that have planter pockets. These can be filled with plants, cacti, or even herbs, and placed in the kitchen. The light adds a nice effect, helps the growing cycle, and permits the growth of culinary edibles.
- Theater lovers and those involved in the performing arts might be attracted to the comedy and tragedy masks. These could make excellent gifts or could go well in recreation rooms or performing arts centers.
- For a child's room or the nursery, select an appropriate TV lamp according to the décor. Young ones love cat, dog, train, and ship themes. Choose appropriate pieces as nightlights and as decorations. Place them on a high shelf for a soft lighting effect.
- Feline lovers and breeders will be bewitched by an assortment of single and double cat lamps.
- Dog owners have numerous lamp styles to attract their attention. Framed photos of their dog(s) and awards can be displayed attractively around their lamps.
- Horse enthusiasts and breeders will be certain to admire colts, racing stallions, and prancing steeds. These lamps were made in a variety of colors and display well-defined muscle tone. Place appropriate horse magazines near the lamps.
- A wife or girlfriend who has a serviceman overseas might be inclined to purchase lamps with such themes as ships, sampans, and Oriental figures. These might have sentimental value for her as she recalls the gifts and scarves sent home by her father to his wife during a war.
- Colonial Conestoga wagons, wheels, and decorative coaches would be quite appropriate for a collector of country and primitive antiques.
- Bird lovers and ornithologists can have fun decorating with bird lamps of any colors and kinds.
- The hunter and fisherman might take a liking to a nice assortment of ducks, fish, deer, and other game. A gallery of mounted wall trophies adds to the mood.
- Female figures would be attractive for the woman of the house. Lamps can enhance the beauty of her bedroom bureau. The lamp pockets could be lined with felt to hold brushes, make-up, combs, perfume, etc.
- The businessman or business woman, or travel agent, might adorn his or her office with one lamp or a diversity of TV lamps. Suitable shapes could be seashells, butterflies, birds of paradise, swans, flowers, and leaves. All seem to suggest peace, contentment, or even a well-deserved vacation to a warmer climate.
- Television lamps might contribute to a festive atmosphere, giving a party an unusual flare. An owl or cat lamp would dress up a Halloween party. Kids would love to be in the presence of a clown or carousel lamp.
- Should your home have an enclosed outdoor porch, this site would accommodate your favorite TV light.
- Motion lamps definitely catch the attention of an infant in a crib. They would also work nicely in a dance or gameroom environment. A fish store or a theme restaurant could create definite conversation starters for its customers through its displays.
- Just mixing or matching TV lamps in a room of your home could create a stunning look.
- TV lamps are appropriate and could be displayed at special affairs or even given as gifts. Think in terms of birthdays, bridal showers, and nationally recognized holidays.
- You can discover appropriate, creative settings for the placement of a lamp or lamps to help create ambience in any home, whether it is one year old or over 200 years old.
- Allow your imaginative side to shine through by the way you display your television lamp collection!

Light green Indian man with planter, 6½" wide, $80.00 – 90.00.

Green and gold Egyptian lady with panther, $100.00 – 110.00.

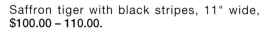

Gray glazed elephant with raised trunk, 11" wide, $80.00 – 90.00.

Saffron tiger with black stripes, 11" wide, $100.00 – 110.00.

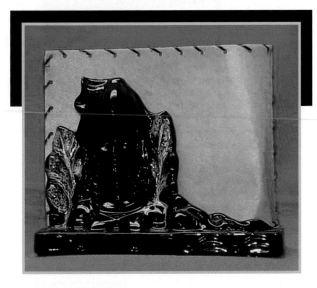

Black African lady in front of fiberglass shield, 9" wide, 8" high, **$85.00 – 95.00.**

Burgundy Egyptian, 8" wide, 10" high, **$80.00 – 90.00.**

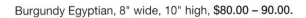

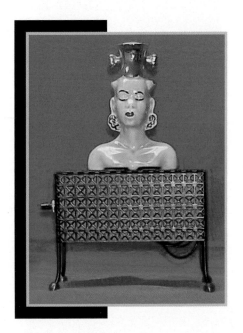

African lady bust, 7" wide, 11½" high, **$100.00 – 110.00.**

Black and yellow African king, 8½" wide, 9" high, **$75.00 – 85.00.**

African queen, shades of black and burgundy, 8" wide, 9" high, **$85.00 – 95.00.**

Zulu African mask, fudge colored, 7" wide, **$150.00 – 165.00.**

Black African head, 9" wide, 12½" high, **$100.00 – 110.00.**

Dark green Royal Haeger Egyptian, 7½" wide, 9½" high, signed "Royal Haeger," **$60.00 – 75.00.**

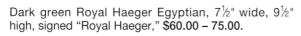

Black and white African royal, 7½" wide, 13" high, **$100.00 – 110.00.**

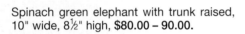

Spinach green elephant with trunk raised, 10" wide, 8½" high, **$80.00 – 90.00.**

Glazed coal black African native with broad golden smile, 9½" wide, **$150.00 – 165.00.**

Pair of airbrushed beige cougars, 11" wide, 12" long, **$150.00 – 160.00.**

Interesting glossy green elephant, 11½" high, 7" wide, signed "Hollywood Eran Hand Made USA," **$85.00 – 95.00.**

Airbrushed tan giraffe among light green foliage, 11" wide, 9" high, gray lined fiberglass shield, **$110.00 – 125.00.**

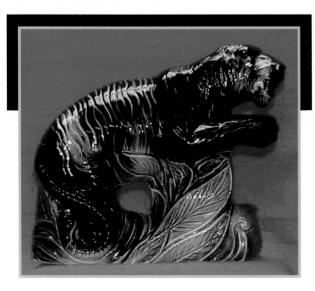

Sinister panther, paw outstretched among the leaves; gray, black, and light green; 10½" wide, 9½" high, **$75.00 – 85.00.**

Glossy black elephant with trunk raised, gold highlights, 7½" wide, 6½" high, **$55.00 – 65.00.**

Dark brown panther with black stripes, 11" wide, 8" high, **$65.00 – 75.00.**

Crouching moss green panther, ceramic, 12" wide, 5" high, **$50.00 – 60.00.**

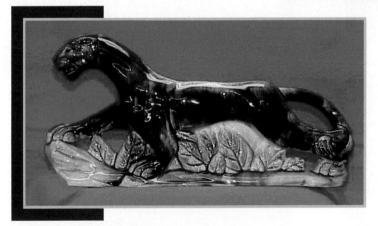

Airbrushed black panther, circa 1950s, light yellow base, 14" wide, 6½" high, **$55.00 – 65.00.**

Glossy airbrushed black panther above a yellow cream decorative ground, 10" wide, 8" high, **$65.00 – 75.00.**

Hazelnut double panthers, 13" wide, 8" high, unique, $85.00 – 95.00.

Light taupe panther on the rocks, 10" wide, 9½" high, $50.00 – 65.00.

Glossy nutmeg panther staring from the rocks, mottled base, 10" wide, 9½" high, $80.00 – 90.00.

Muscular black panther mounted on a rectangular base showing eight crackle white disks, 16" wide, 8½" high, signed "Kron," $85.00 – 95.00.

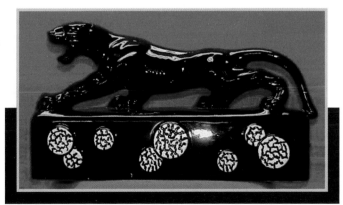

Two moss green gazelles, 13½" wide, 11½" high, **$65.00 – 75.00.**

Light lime green running gazelle, circa 1950s, 11½" wide, 11" high, **$55.00 – 75.00.**

Climbing golden goat on a spinach green ground, 7½" wide, 9" high, **$55.00 – 70.00.**

Broccoli green running gazelle, 14" wide, 10½" high, **$65.00 – 75.00.**

Kiwi green 1950s gazelle, 10" wide, 13" high, **$65.00 – 75.00.**

Large black panther glaring from the rocks, circa 1959, 15" wide, 12½" high, signed "Lane Van Nuys, Calif. USA.," **$100.00 – 110.00.**

Green panther with planter, 10½" wide, 5" high, **$45.00 – 60.00.**

Light yellow-green crouching panther, 20½" wide, 5" high, **$75.00 – 85.00.**

Shiny licorice black crouching panther, with planter, 20½" wide, 5" high, marked "Royal China Novelty Co., Inc.," $75.00 – 85.00.

Tobacco brown crouching panther, 20" wide, 5" high, $65.00 – 75.00.

Lime green gold-striped panther, 15½" wide, 4½" high, $65.00 – 75.00.

Coal black panther lurking on airbrushed rocks, 15½" wide, 10½" high, signed "Lane Van Nuys 1959," $80.00 – 95.00.

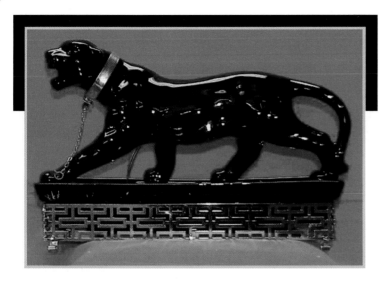

Midnight black stalking panther with brass collar, chain, and ankle bracelet, 15½" wide, 10½" high, $100.00 – 125.00.

Reclining licorice black panther, 18½" wide, 7" high, $200.00 – 225.00.

Coal black panther standing on his hind legs, 6½" wide, 15" high, $350.00 – 375.00.

Glossy black panther looking over his shoulder, 13½" wide, 9½" high, $100.00 – 115.00.

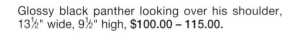

Regal and elaborate satin black, white, and gold African woman's head, 7½" wide, 11½" high, **$85.00 – 95.00.**

Intertwined watermelon green giraffes, 10½" wide, 12½" high, **$100.00 – 125.00.**

Iridescent black and bronze arched-neck panther, 11" wide, 13" high, **$80.00 – 95.00.**

Glaring shiny black panther on an airbrushed base, 11½" wide, 10½" high, signed "Lane Van Nuys 1959," **$85.00 – 95.00.**

Crouching lime green panther, 9" wide, 7" high, **$25.00 – 35.00.**

Two charcoal gray and black zebras, green highlights on the base, 11" wide, 10" high, **$125.00 – 135.00.**

Fudge brown elephant with trunk lifted, yellow ears, 11" wide, 9½" high, **$80.00 – 95.00.**

Yellow-green elephant, ceramic, 1950s, 11" wide, 8" high, **$80.00 – 95.00.**

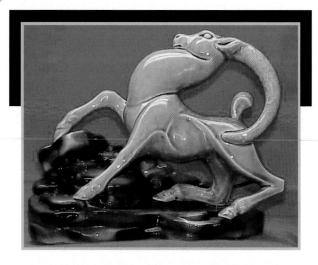

Light tan gazelle on a green and yellow base, 10½" wide, 9" high, **$75.00 – 90.00.**

Striking glossy running zebra with wide gold stripes and frontal gold hues, 12" wide, 9" high, **$110.00 – 125.00.**

Zebra with black stripes on snow white base, laced back of tan fiberglass, 9½" wide, 7½" high, **$75.00 – 95.00.**

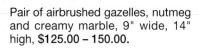

Pair of airbrushed gazelles, nutmeg and creamy marble, 9" wide, 14" high, **$125.00 – 150.00.**

Shiny coal black panther, pyramid-shaped cardinal red metal shade, two open front pockets, 10" wide, 20" high, **$100.00 – 125.00.**

Shiny black curled-tail stalking panther, displays stylized red and yellow tulip-like flowers, 16" wide, 10" high, **$100.00 – 125.00.**

Black panther on marble green and black base, tail curled under, panther looking over his shoulder, backlighted, 10" wide, 12¾" high, **$75.00 – 90.00.**

Garnet crouching panther, front planter, backlighted, 8½" wide, 6½" high, **$50.00 – 65.00.**

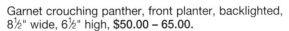

Black panther with green jeweled eyes, tan and rust brown, backlighted, candy dish in front, 14" wide, 10½" high, **$125.00 – 150.00.**

Black panther with curly tail, by "Kron, Bangs, Texas," dual planter in front, 15" wide, 9" high, **$85.00 – 100.00.**

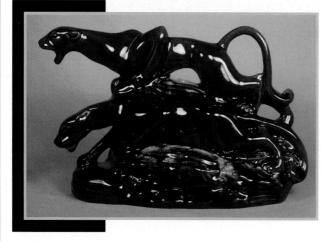

Chocolate brown stalking cougars, tan glaze, 12" wide, 8½" high, **$100.00 – 125.00.**

Crouching tiger on a log, tobacco stain and hazelnut glazes, black leaves and stripes, 9½" wide, 8" high, **$85.00 – 100.00.**

Bronzed hunting panther with great muscle tone, on crags, caramel drippings, backlighted, 10½" wide, 13" high, **$100.00 – 125.00.**

Shiny tan glaring panther on rocky formation, back planter, 12" wide, 9½" high, **$100.00 – 125.00.**

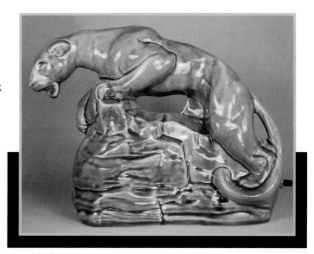

Shiny midnight black stalking panther, wisps of marbleized green, front planter, backlighted, 17" wide, 8" high, **$85.00 – 100.00.**

Coal black crouching panther on rocky base, backlighted, 6" wide, 10" high, **$65.00 – 85.00.**

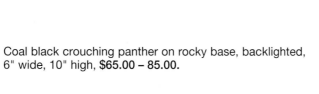

Chartreuse panther with green jeweled eyes, brass base, black collar with chain, signed "Lane & Co., LA Cal © 1953," 16" wide, 11" high, **$75.00 – 90.00.**

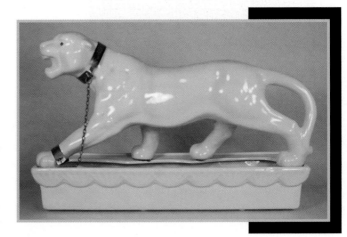

Sheer yellow cougar planter with light, brass collar and chain with leg cuff, green jeweled eyes, 15" wide, 9½" high, signed "LANE & Co LA. Calif. © 1953," brass base missing, **$70.00 – 80.00.**

Hershey chocolate stalking panther, eyes light, backlighted, hues of black, white, tan, and chartreuse; 22" wide, 4½" high, **$65.00 – 85.00.**

Burgundy crouching panther, front planter, backlighted, 8½" wide, 6½" high, **$50.00 – 65.00.**

Black panther, white marble swirls on the leaves and base, double front planter, backlighted, 15" wide, **$75.00 – 85.00.**

Close-up of previous photo.

Shiny coal black crouched panther, green jeweled eyes, sprayed green and tan base, backlighted, 16" wide, 13" high, **$125.00 – 140.00.**

Iridescent and marbleized green stylish giraffes, Royal Haeger, lighted with back screen, 9" wide, 16" high, **$150.00 – 175.00.**

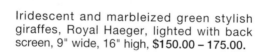

Shiny licorice black elephant, backlighted, 10" wide, 7¼" high, **$65.00 – 75.00.**

Shiny elephant with chocolate and tan drippings, backlighted, 10" wide, 7¼" high, $65.00 – 75.00.

Glossy nutmeg elephant, tan and lime green ears, curled marble highlighted trunk, back-lighted, 10½" wide, 9½" high, $70.00 – 95.00.

Apple green/light green and ivory Deco gazelle on a six-scrolled base, 13" wide, 10¼" high, $75.00 – 95.00.

Ornate Art Deco reclining gazelle, shiny nutmeg glaze, lime and tan highlights, backlighted, 11¾" wide, 14" high, $75.00 – 90.00.

Licorice black running gazelle with verde waves and highlights, 13" wide, 9½" high, **$75.00 – 90.00.**

Charcoal green running gazelle on wavy grass, 13" wide, 9½" high, **$75.00 – 90.00.**

Green briar reclining gazelle, serrated basket planter in the back, unsigned Royal Haeger, 16" wide, 8" high, **$150.00 – 175.00.**

Marbleized black and jade green leaping gazelles, double front planter, 13½" wide, 11½" high, **$100.00 – 125.00.**

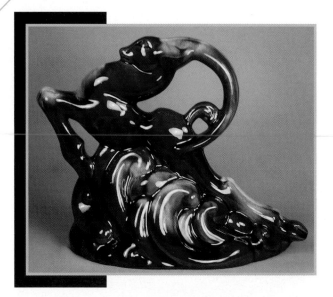

Leaping Art Deco gazelle, marbleized hazelnut brown and yellowish melon green, 11" wide, 10" high, **$100.00 – 125.00.**

Charcoal black marbleized leaping gazelle, planter and backlight, 14" wide, 11" high, **$125.00 – 140.00.**

Amber-finish gazelle, marbleized base, back planter and light, 18" wide, 14" high, **$125.00 – 140.00.**

Green gazelle, back planter and light, 18" wide, 14" high, **$125.00 – 150.00.**

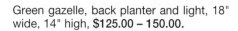

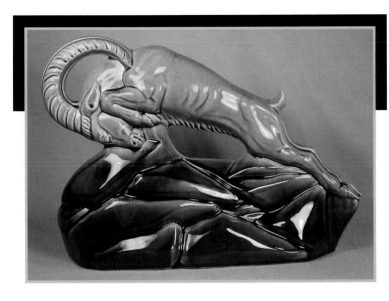

Antique tan butting gazelle on geometric rock shapes, moss green base, 15" wide, 10½" high, **$150.00 – 175.00.**

Striated green prancing gazelle, sculptured front, backlighted, dual front planter, 15" wide, 10" high, **$85.00 – 100.00.**

Shiny coal black panther against a gnarled tree, original laced oval Oriental red shade, 12" diameter, 26" high, **$95.00 – 115.00.**

M
A
T
A
D
O
R
S

&

B
U
L
L
S

Matador fighting a bull; tan, black, yellow, and red; 13" wide, **$125.00 – 135.00.**

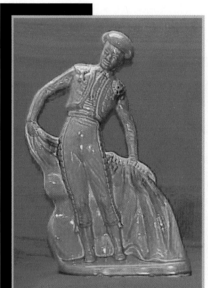

Mustard-tinted matador, 15½" high, came with original packaging, signed "Lane and Co Van Nuys, Calif USA," **$80.00 – 90.00.**

Matador with cape, 9" wide, 15½" high, signed "Lane and Co., 1959," **$100.00 – 110.00.**

Light tan Brahman bull with raised hump, 12" wide, 10" high, **$175.00 – 190.00.**

Detailed three-dimensional fireplace, 12" wide, 9" high, signed "Lane L-2010," **$100.00 – 110.00.**

Green fireplace, ceramic, 8" high, signed "McCoy," with original packaging, **$75.00 – 85.00.**

Adorable airbrushed figures, Jack jumping over the candlestick, 8" wide, **$150.00 – 165.00.**

Glazed woman Toby mug on a wooden base, 8" wide, 9" high, with original packaging, marked "Sawage of Calif.," **$110.00 – 125.00.**

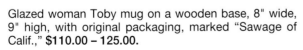

Colorful airbrushed Toby jug; colonial man wearing tri-corner hat, rectangular glasses, and wig; 6" wide, $80.00 – 95.00.

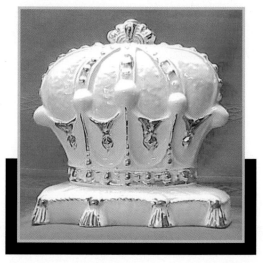

Fancy white crown on a pillow, gold highlights, ceramic, 9" wide, $75.00 – 85.00.

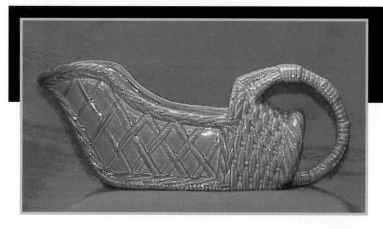

Golden wine bottle basket holder with handle, 14" wide, $50.00 – 60.00.

Pink ceramic genie lamp, gold flame, 14" wide, 6½" high, $75.00 – 85.00.

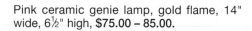

Brown and yellow mottled-glaze cornucopia basket with handle, 13" wide, 7" high, **$55.00 – 65.00.**

Light pink globe, continents highlighted with gold, 8" wide, 11" high, **$75.00 – 85.00.**

Green miniature TV with matching planters, all pieces on metal stands, 19" wide, 10" high, **$140.00 – 150.00.**

Scarce white pitcher and bowl set, 12" wide, 10½" high, marked "Lane & Co., Van Nuys, Calif., L-2011," **$60.00 – 75.00.**

Smiling open-armed brown and white bear, circa 1950s, 8½" wide, 10½" high, signed "Kron," **$100.00 – 125.00.**

Incised mark "LANE & CO. VAN NUYS, CALIF., U.S.A. P80 © 1959."

Original red and white Maddux paper label "825 1 lb. swan planter white PK. Ind. 5# Retail Price $7.00 ea. 11 x 13 x 6."

Back of Haeger paper label.

Front of Haeger paper label.

Bronzed Haeger ceramic sign, 8½" wide, 2½" high, **$85.00 – 100.00.**

Pillared and stained light maple clock and TV lamp, round "United" clock with cast metal logs and andirons, decorative flowers and leaves, tan parchment coloration, marked "UNITED CLOCK CORP. BROOKLYN, NEW YORK MODEL NO. 419," 10½" wide, 8½" high, **$100.00 – 125.00.**

Snow white semicircular planter, gold spattered, scalloped edge, signed "MADDUX OF CALIF. LOS ANGELES #3006," mounted in cut-out floral brass frame, backlighted, 10" wide, 5½" high, **$45.00 – 55.00.**

Charcoal-toned semicircular planter with raised ivy design, fancy designed base, backlighted, marked "Gilner" on the base of the planter, 11¼" wide, 6½" high, **$45.00 – 60.00.**

"Home Sweet Home" light and clock, hazelnut plastic with gray roof, marked "A Haddon Original, Chicago 8, Ill.," fireplace and top window light, grandmother rocks back and forth, **$110.00 – 125.00.**

Classy airbrushed Oriental, red, pink, gray, and white hues; 7" wide, marked "Navis and Smith Co., Chicago, Ill.," **$85.00 – 95.00.**

Glazed platinum stylish woman with necklace, woman wears crown and has long hair, 8" wide, **$100.00 – 125.00.**

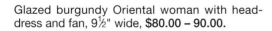

Glazed and painted Oriental boy and girl against a wavy background, stark black trees with foliage; children colored white, red, and black; 10" wide, **$100.00 – 110.00.**

Glazed burgundy Oriental woman with head-dress and fan, 9½" wide, **$80.00 – 90.00.**

Glazed light yellow figure reclining against a basket, 8½" high, **$80.00 – 90.00.**

Glazed Asian couple with a bird, watermelon green front dish, geometric brass base and lighting shell, green fiberglass interior for bulb placement, 13" wide, **$150.00 – 160.00.**

Robed lime green figure with mandolin standing in a dark green entranceway, 8" wide, 12" high, **$85.00 – 95.00.**

Raised green airbrushed dragon on a white tapered vase, 6" wide, 10½" high, original packaging, Miramar of California, **$55.00 – 65.00.**

Burgundy glazed raised dragon on a tapered pedestal vase, gold trim, 6" wide, 10½" high, original packaging, labeled "Miramar of Calif Walsco TVL," $55.00 – 65.00.

Light turquoise girl on a bridge, creamy white figural laced screen, 9½" wide, $55.00 – 65.00.

Boy in glazed white archway highlighted in gold, 11½" wide, $100.00 – 110.00.

Colorful glazed couple sitting on a decorative wall, elaborate silver mesh screen is the central focal point, 12" wide, $80.00 – 90.00.

Detailed open fan, white with blue and gold decorative tints, 14" wide, 9" high, $55.00 – 65.00.

Two figures on a sampan, airbrushed, glazed, mottled accents, 13½" wide, 5" high, "Premco Mfg. Co., 1954, Chicago, Ill.," $80.00 – 95.00.

Airbrushed Oriental couple on glossy black sampan trimmed in gold, 15" wide, 7" high, $75.00 – 95.00.

Lovely and serene Oriental woman in a garden of cherry blossoms, hand-painted and glazed colors, 12" wide, 8½" high, $65.00 – 75.00.

Regal robed and reclining Oriental woman, glossy white glaze, 11½" wide, 13" high, marked "Maddux of Calif.," **$110.00 – 125.00.**

Oriental woman depicted in black, white, gold, and red, silhouetted in front of a chartreuse open fan, 10" wide, 12" high, **$90.00 – 100.00.**

Burgundy glazed male military figure, 9½" wide, 10½" high, **$85.00 – 95.00.**

Enticing airbrushed Oriental home among a flower garden, 14" wide, 9½" high, "Lane and Co., Van Nuys Made in USA.," **$110.00 – 125.00.**

Light green figure on a bridge surrounded by a darker green vegetation, 13" wide, 11½" high, $85.00 – 95.00.

Ornate ivory sampan trimmed in gold carrying Chinese couple, double top planters, internally lighted windows, marked "© PREMCO MFG. CO., Chicago, Ill 1954," $70.00 – 90.00.

Close-up of one figure from previous photograph.

Plaster-of-Paris Oriental couple next to a wishing well, backlighted; colored flat back, ivory, spattered shades of green; 13" wide, 9" high, signed "Silvestri Bros. © Pat 174,101," $125.00 – 140.00.

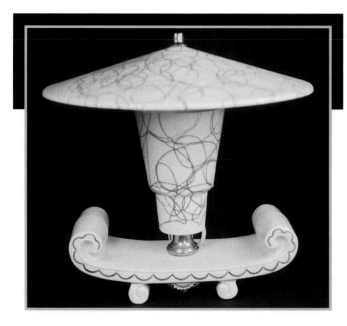

Shiny dark cream lamp, lighted internally, scrolled base and feet, golden highlights, fiberglass body and shade with impressed curly red strings, 10" wide, 9½" high, new with original box and packaging, box marked "ROCK ISLAND, ILLINOIS, MODEL 68," $85.00 – 95.00.

Lamp view from above.

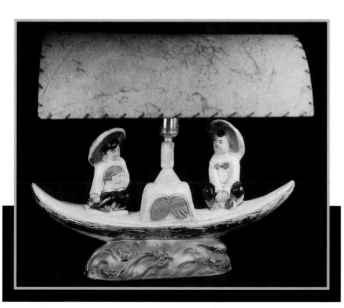

Pair of Oriental figures sitting on a chalk white plaster-of-Paris sampan; airbrushed gold, black, and flesh tones; original clamp on curved parchment-hued and laced fiberglass shade, 17½" wide, 16" high, $175.00 – 200.00.

CLEANING AND RESTORING TV LAMPS

Lamps that are purchased may need some help to make them sparkle and be safe to use and display.

Mild liquid detergent, warm water, and a sponge will aid in removing years of built-up grime. Q-tips and toothpicks are helpful for getting into small cracks and crevices. Ammonia and denatured alcohol are also good cleaning agents. Allow the lamp to dry on a draining board. Complete the drying task with soft flannel and terrycloth.

An alternative, easier, and safer method for cleaning your TV lamps was offered by Mr. and Mrs. Parks while we were photographing their collection.

Place your lamp in the sink on a towel or rubber mat for safety. Cover the bulb socket with a clear plastic lunch bag, and tape securely. Run the unplugged electrical cord out of the way along the flat sink surface. Spray the lamp with Woolite Fabric & Upholstery Foam Cleaner. Permit the lamp to stand for a few minutes until completely dry. Watch how your TV light is revived and takes on a new look.

This process will work for all lamps. But it is especially beneficial for those having colored pressed glass flowers. These flowers are very fragile and attached by copper wires covered with silk, so take your time and do not rush the process.

Periodically your collection can be made to look like new again. Settled dust may be removed with a feather duster or a vacuum cleaner. Use the small brush attachment and turn the dial of the cleaner to a low setting.

Lamps may require new felt on their bases so that they do not slide and scratch pieces of furniture. Felt squares may be used on the bases of smaller lamps. They usually sell for about 20 cents each and come in numerous colors that match the lamps. Available are white, chocolate, tan, light and dark green, red, pink, ivory, and mustard.

Trace a matching pattern from the lamps to be restored. Cut each piece of felt precisely, so that it fits the lamp base properly. Join the felt and the lamp with adhesives such as rubber cement or "Real Deal" Tacky Glue. Both sell for about $1.00 each.

Felt by the yard is also available. It sells for around $5.00 per yard and comes in the following shades: white, ivory, purple, cardinal red, royal blue, black, bright yellow, salmon, and forest green.

PROTECTING YOUR COLLECTION

Get a bill of sale marked "paid" for each TV lamp that you purchase. Keep an accurate file of all transactions.

Record the date, price, dealer's name and address, and an accurate description of each lamp. Include themes, measurements, company logos, paper labels, and any other recognizable pertinent features.

Keep a visual record using colored photos, slides, transparencies, or digital memory disks. Label each image for clarity.

Include your TV lamps, along with other antiques/collectibles and fine arts, on your insurance policy. You are most interested in replacement value in case of fire and water damage, theft, breakage, etc.

Hire a certified and bonded appraiser to provide you with a written evaluation of all the lamps in your collection.

Add this list along with colored images to a fine arts binder on your insurance policy. Keep three separate records — one at home in a secure place, one in a bank vault, and one with your insurance agent.

Also make provisions in your will as to the inheritance specifics at the time of your death. Make certain that you have outlined and assigned guardianship and power of attorney duties to reliable and trustworthy individuals.

Should you wish to dispose of your TV lamps before your demise, try flea markets, cooperatives, a house auction, a catalog sale, eBay, newspaper ads, or a donation to a historical society or museum.

Special events also make for pleasant, surprising times to share your collection with loved ones, including immediate family and relatives. Designate a specific date such as a birthday, a marriage, a baptism, a graduation, Christmas, New Year's, Valentine's Day, St. Patrick's Day, Easter, or another specific time, or be spontaneous.

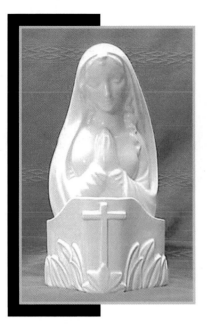

White bust of Madonna praying, cross in the foreground, circa 1950s, 6" wide, $55.00 – 65.00.

Plaster-of-Paris airbrushed topaz figure of Christ, gilded cross that lights, "GOD BLESS OUR HOME," marked "COPYRIGHT 1960 — SILVESTRI BROS. — PATENT PENDING," 10½" wide, 15" high, $95.00 – 110.00.

Oval scalloped green and yellow bowl with wired pressed multicolored leaves and flowers, crucifixion of Christ in the background, 7" wide, 12½" high, $65.00 – 75.00.

Reproduction iridescent "Han Jin Co.," Japanese molded plastic TV and prayer lamp, shows two swans, both lighted internally, marked "Rejoice Always!", 6½" wide, 10½" high, $30.00 – 40.00.

Snow white aquarium with foliage that becomes visible when the lamp is turned on, 12" wide, **$55.00 – 65.00.**

Light pink ribbed shell, 8" wide, 7" high, **$65.00 – 75.00.**

Realistic-looking conch shell, circa 1950s, 13" wide, 6½" high, **$75.00 – 85.00.**

Green fish and black fish, ceramic, 11" wide, 12" high, marked "Calif.," **$100.00 – 110.00.**

Light green ceramic grinding mill house with water wheel, 11" wide, 9½" high, $100.00 – 110.00.

Tan and green seaweed, 9½" wide, 8½" high, $75.00 – 85.00.

Pink-hued Royal Haeger angelfish, 8" wide, 14" high, marked with an original paper label, also has the original packaging, $155.00 – 175.00.

Pair of murky green angelfish, 10" wide, 10" high, marked "Gilner," $75.00 – 85.00.

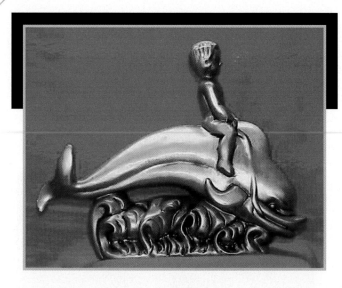

Golden boy on a golden dolphin, 15½" wide, 12" high, labeled "Lane and Co., Van Nuys, Calif., USA.," $125.00 – 140.00.

Malachite arched sailfish, 9¼" wide, 10" high, $75.00 – 85.00.

Double fish, ceramic, 1950s, 8" wide, 10" high, $75.00 – 85.00.

Jumping lime green sailfish, golden accents, 12" wide, 11" high, $75.00 – 85.00.

Four white dolphins playing, green and black highlights, 9" wide, 12" high, $100.00 – 125.00.

Elongated ceramic fish, 21" wide, 5" high, marked "C. Miller 1956," $80.00 – 90.00.

Ivy green angelfish in front of fiberglass screen, 13½" wide, 10" high, **$100.00 – 125.00.**

Pair of blowfish on a decorative base, 10½" wide, 7" high, **$55.00 – 65.00.**

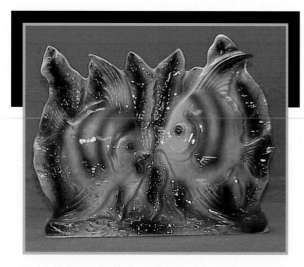

Bright yellow pair of angelfish, green and black accents, 9" wide, 7" high, **$75.00 – 85.00.**

Airbrushed angelfish playing among leaves, vibrant colors, 7" wide, 7" high, **$70.00 – 85.00.**

Mysterious black and gold angelfish, 9" wide, 10½" high, **$70.00 – 80.00.**

Light green lustered fish, 13" wide, 7½" high, **$55.00 – 65.00.**

Frolicking long-haired smoke gray mermaid, 12" wide, 8" high, $85.00 – 95.00.

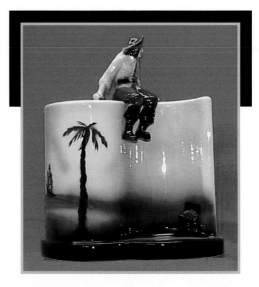

Artistic ceramic lamp showing wave, pirate, ship, beach, and trees, 12" wide, 13" high, $125.00 – 135.00.

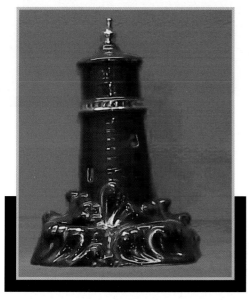

Emerald green lighthouse, highlighted with gold, 8" wide, 12" high, $65.00 – 75.00.

Lime green mermaid sitting in front of fiberglass screen, 10" wide, 8" high, $65.00 – 75.00.

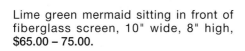

Pink seashell, 13" wide, 7" high, $65.00 – 75.00.

Light silver aspen cornucopia, airbrushed, nine lobes in the green shell, $45.00 – 55.00.

Glossy cream and green nine-lobed shell, 9" wide, 9½" high, $75.00 – 85.00.

Ceramic aqua green shell, bulb inside makes the gold highlighted web glow, 10" wide, 8" high, marked "Premco Mfg. Co., CHEO 1950," $85.00 – 95.00.

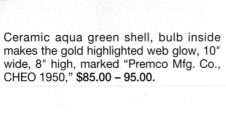

Ceramic light blue shell, circa 1950s, 8"
wide, 11" high, **$70.00 – 90.00.**

Green and gold ceramic shell, 8" wide, 8"
high, **$70.00 – 90.00.**

Apple green tropical fish, front planter, 10"
wide, 13½" high, **$100.00 – 110.00.**

Graceful white six-lobed shell, 8½" wide,
8" high, **$35.00 – 45.00.**

Glossy sable gnarled tree trunk, 10" wide, 10½" high, **$45.00 – 55.00.**

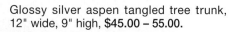

Glossy silver aspen tangled tree trunk, 12" wide, 9" high, **$45.00 – 55.00.**

Colorful 1950s double-towered castle, 7" wide, 11" high, **$60.00 – 75.00.**

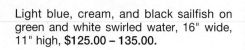

Light blue, cream, and black sailfish on green and white swirled water, 16" wide, 11" high, **$125.00 – 135.00.**

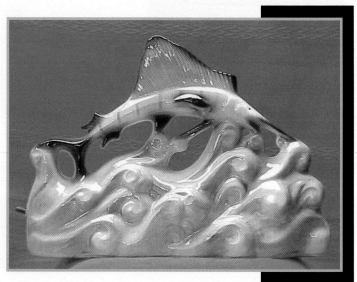

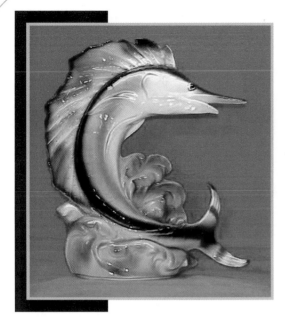

Airbrushed jumping sailfish, rainbow hues on pink and green water, 10½" wide, 12" high, signed "Lane Van Nuys, Calif.," **$75.00 – 90.00.**

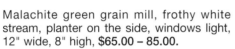

Malachite green grain mill, frothy white stream, planter on the side, windows light, 12" wide, 8" high, **$65.00 – 85.00.**

Marbleized green sailfish, 11" long, 14½" high, backlighted, **$125.00 – 150.00.**

Haeger iridescent jade green triple leaping fish, dripped blue-green waves, rear planter and light, 13" wide, 13" high, **$65.00 – 75.00.**

Stylized tea rose fish light and planter, backlighted, spattered with gold, 10½" wide, 8½" high, signed "MARCIA OF CALIF.," $85.00 – 95.00.

Burgundy sailfish, Haeger, 10½" wide, 10½" high, $85.00 – 95.00.

Iridescent omelet yellow tropical fish, black purple eyes, clear jewels throughout, lighted internally, crystal nose, 10" wide, 12" high, **$100.00 – 125.00.**

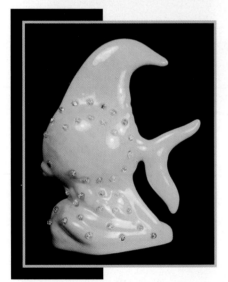

Colorful and iridescent plaster-of-Paris lamp showing two pink starfish, seven shells, white coral, and two periwinkle blue swordfish, 8" wide, 6" high, **$60.00 – 75.00.**

Marbleized plaster-of-Paris shell art lamp with large back iridescent shell, seven other assorted shells, pink coral, and cameo rose plastic flamingo, sailing ship with rigging, 8" diameter, 7" high, **$60.00 – 75.00.**

Hollow molded plaster-of-Paris airbrushed lighthouse with the addition of a house, dog, and boat, lighted internally, shows numerous colors, 10½" wide, 16" high, **$65.00 – 75.00.**

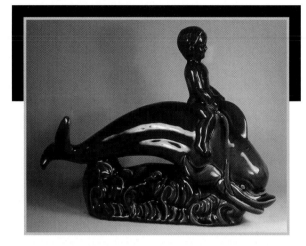

Shiny moss green nude youth holding two reins and riding a plump dolphin with a curved tail, backlighted, signed "LANE & CO. VAN NUYS, CALIF. U.S.A. © 8527," 15½" long, 11½" high, **$125.00 – 140.00.**

Close-up of the boy from the previous photo.

Light cream and cranberry marbleized plaster-of-Paris base, large shell in the background, lighted internally; foreground shows shells, coral, and plastic Persian blue parakeet; 8½" diameter, 8" high, **$60.00 – 75.00.**

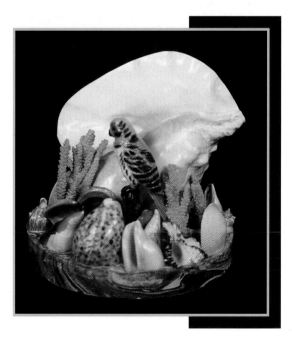

Close-up.

TELEVISION TIMELINE

- July 30, 1930 — NBC began operating an experimental TV station in New York City (W2XBS).
- July 21, 1931 — CBS began a regular schedule of broadcasting in New York City on W2XAB.
- October 30, 1931 — NBC began experimental TV broadcasts from the top of the Empire State Building in New York City.
- April 30, 1939 — NBC introduced TV as a regular service. Franklin D. Roosevelt was the first president to be seen on TV.
- June 24, 1940 — A coaxial cable was installed between New York and Philadelphia.
- October 27, 1940 — The first experimental color was broadcast from CBS in New York City.
- 1941 — The first transmitters commercially licensed in New York City were stations WNBT and WCBW.
- October 25, 1945 — The image orthicon tube was introduced.
- September 17, 1946 — The first postwar TV sets went on sale.
- January 3, 1947 — First Congressional session was telecast from Washington.
- January 20, 1949 — The inauguration of President Truman was seen on 15 stations from St. Louis to Boston.
- May 11, 1949 — First color telecast of a surgical operation was broadcast from the University of Pennsylvania hospital in Philadelphia.
- September 4, 1951 — TV broadcast showing President Truman opening the Japanese Peace Treaty Conference, San Francisco, was aired coast to coast.
- 1952 — The Democratic/Republican national conventions were televised nationwide for the first time.
- October 31, 1953 — Electronic color was used in an hour program.
- January 1, 1954 — The Rose Bowl Parade in Pasadena, California, was telecast nationwide.
- 1954 — Swanson Frozen Foods Co. introduced the TV dinner. According to a segment on *Curious World*, Mr. Gerry Thomas, an employee, got an idea for a three-compartment TV tray. The food was heated and then enjoyed under the light of the TV lamp as one watched his or her favorite program. Thomas was awarded a $1,000 bonus by Swanson for his idea. The tray was placed in production and continues to be popular today. The original tray is on display in the Thomas home in Paradise Valley, Arizona.
- January 19, 1955 — The first motion pictures of a presidential press conference were shown on TV.
- May 12, 1955 — A tape recording of a color TV program was transmitted over closed circuit from New York City to Saint Paul, Minnesota.

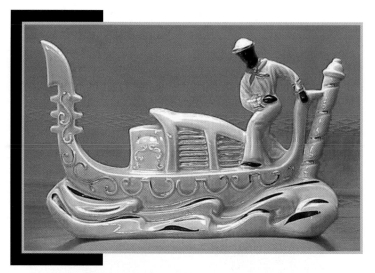

Chartreuse gondola and gondolier, 14" wide, 9" high, **$75.00 – 95.00.**

Light tan ship with metal sails, portholes light, 17" wide, 15½" high, **$75.00 – 90.00.**

Fudge brown ceramic ship, 11" wide, 13½" high, **$75.00 – 90.00.**

Tobacco brown sailing ship, 15" wide, 13" high, **$75.00 – 90.00.**

Subtle black and gold Maddux ship, 12" wide, 12½" high, signed "Maddux of Calif. #806," $70.00 – 80.00.

Yellow-green Nordic ship, tan accents, 12" wide, 9½" high, $75.00 – 90.00.

Crisp white and gold sailing ship, circa 1950s, 11" wide, 10½" high, $65.00 – 85.00.

Subdued white ceramic ship, tan body, aqua waves, 11" wide, 11½" high, by Maddux, $75.00 – 85.00.

Unusual black and gold Hawaiian girl in a canoe, 13" wide, 9" high, signed "Alden Hollywood Productions #E 21588," $65.00 – 75.00.

Nordic airbrushed ship, pink and chalk white, 12" wide, 9½" high, $75.00 – 95.00.

Ceramic sailboat, 7½" wide, 10½" high, $55.00 – 65.00.

Small sailboat on a green and white decorative ground, 9" wide, 12" high, $55.00 – 65.00.

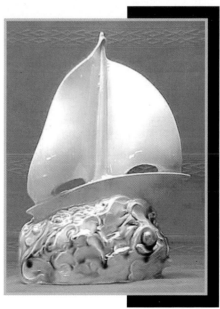

Black and gold boat with man aboard, 16" wide, 7½" high, gold accents, $50.00 – 60.00.

Mustard yellow Norse ship, airbrushed highlights, 12" wide, 9½" high, $45.00 – 55.00.

Black and gold riverboat, circa 1950s, 15" wide, 7" high, $70.00 – 90.00.

Lime green ship showing sails and gold highlights, by Lampcraft China, with original box/packaging/paperwork, 12" wide, 10½" high, $55.00 – 75.00.

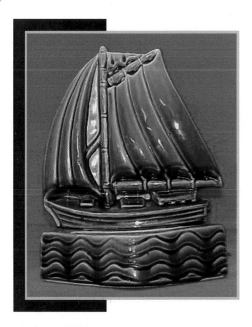

Glossy ivy green ship with sails, 7" wide,
9" high, $65.00 – 75.00.

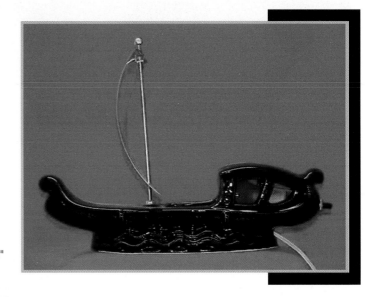

Glossy black Oriental boat with mast, 15"
wide, 10" high, $45.00 – 55.00.

Detailed chalk white pirate ship, 11" wide,
9½" high, $65.00 – 75.00.

Creamy white sailing ship with black and burgundy
detailing, 11" wide, 11" high, $55.00 – 65.00.

Black Egyptian boat, circa 1950s, 10" wide, 5" high, **$65.00 – 85.00.**

Mustard yellow Chinese boat with sail, 13" wide, 10½" high, **$70.00 – 80.00.**

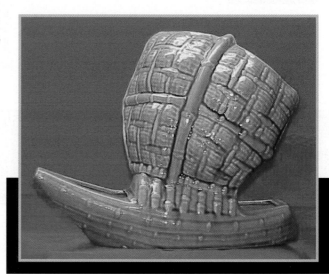

Glossy licorice black ship with light-up portals, gold décor, 10" wide, 9½" high, **$75.00 – 85.00.**

Mustard gold galleon, black rampant lion on the sail, black waves, backlighted through the sail, 11½" wide, 9¾" high, **$80.00 – 90.00.**

Molded cast iron galleon with cutouts, gilded with black and green staining, a bright red clip holds chipped glass disk, backlighted, diameter of the disk 8", ship measures 9½" wide and 9" high, **$85.00 – 100.00.**

Shiny malachite galleon with three portholes, lighted internally, two decorative pressed-aluminum sails, 10" wide, 9" high, **$75.00 – 90.00.**

1950s TELEVISION PERSONALITIES & POPULAR SHOWS

Quality TV programming and talented stars brought the world into the living room. Televisions in the 1950s had small round screens, and pictures were dark. Colored plastics were placed over the picture tube in an effort to give the image more color and vibrance.

A better idea was in the offering, as manufacturers were creating a great variety of TV lamps that provided backlighting. The lamps became very popular and were in vogue almost ten years.

Popular television shows and stars included the following:

- The Smothers Brothers
- Sid Caesar
- Imogene Coco
- Walter Cronkite
- The Rolling Stones
- Jackie Gleason
- The Kennedy vs. Nixon Debate
- Jack Paar
- Bert Parks
- Groucho Marx
- Danny Thomas
- Dean Martin
- Jerry Lewis
- Bob Hope
- Jack Benny
- Jimmy Durante
- Abbot and Costello
- Phil Silvers
- William Bendix
- Shirley Temple
- *The Lone Ranger*
- *Quiz Kids*
- The Goldbergs

- *Original Amateur Hour*
- *Your Show Of Shows*
- *The Garry Moore Show*
- *The Kate Smith Hour*
- *The Steve Allen Show*
- *What's My Line?*
- *Captain Video And His Video Rangers*
- *The George Burns-Grade Alien Show*
- *Truth or Consequences*
- *I Love Lucy*
- *The Roy Rogers Show*
- *The Jack LaLanne Show*
- *Search for Tomorrow*
- *Hopalong Cassidy*
- *Milton Berle Texaco Show*
- *Cavalcade of Stars*
- *M*A*S*H*
- *The Mary Tyler Moore Show*
- *Father Knows Best*
- *The Cosby Show*
- *The Simpsons*

- *Amos 'n Andy*
- *Mama*
- *The Life of Riley*
- *The Donna Reed Show*
- *The Howdy Doody Show*
- *The Beverly Hillbillies*
- *The Rocky and Bullwinkle Show*
- *Candid Camera*
- *The Jimmy Durante Show*
- *The Andy Griffith Show*
- *The Honeymooners*
- *The Tonight Show*
- *The Little Rascals*
- *The Adventures of Ozzie And Harriet*
- Perry Mason
- *The Red Skelton Show*
- *The Twilight Zone*
- *The Lawrence Welk Show*
- *Your Hit Parade*
- *American Bandstand* *

* On July 9, 1956, Dick Clark became the host of an afternoon dance show for teenagers. The show ran until 1989 and profoundly influenced the history of rock and roll and youth culture. This TV show was filmed live on Market Street in Philadelphia, Pennsylvania, from WFIL-TV's Studio B.

Records and stars were introduced to which teens danced. Clark had the ability to make a record an instant hit and a person an instant star.

Some who appeared on the show include: Connie Francis, Danny and the Juniors, Don and Phil Everly, Jerry Lee Lewis, Johnny Mathis, Frankie Avalon, Fabian, Bobby Rydell, Brenda Lee, Chubby Checker, the Supremes, the Osmonds, Led Zeppelin, John Travolta, Madonna, and a host of others.

Gray and black steam locomotive, 14" wide, signed "Claes copyright '54," **$150.00 – 165.00.**

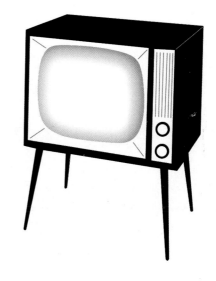

Light brown coach with horses and driver, 8½" wide, 7" high, marked "Japan," **$75.00 – 85.00.**

Cream-colored coach, marked "Japan," 10" wide, 7" high, **$50.00 – 60.00.**

Fancy black and gold Cinderella coach, 13" wide, 9" high, **$75.00 – 85.00.**

White coach enhanced with gilding, 13" wide, 9" high, signed "Japan," **$75.00 – 85.00.**

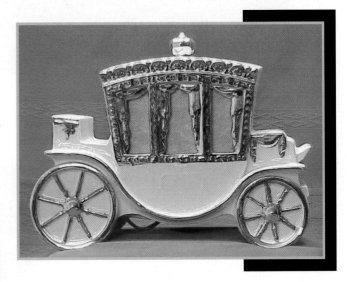

Carousel coach with horses and riders, 10" wide, 7" high, **$75.00 – 85.00.**

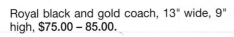

Royal black and gold coach, 13" wide, 9" high, **$75.00 – 85.00.**

Light green antique convertible, with planter, 10" wide, marked "Buckingham," $45.00 – 55.00.

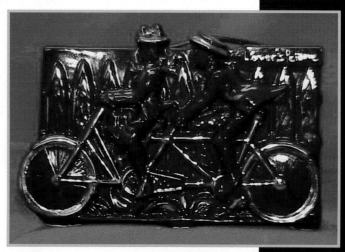

Dark green bicycle built for two, "Lover's Lane" and other details highlighted with gold, 9½" wide, $55.00 – 65.00.

Light brown ceramic car with wire wheels, 14" wide, 6½" high, $75.00 – 85.00.

Burgundy two-door coupe, 9" wide, 6" high, $50.00 – 60.00.

Unusual crackle-glazed gold car, 9" wide,
6" high, $65.00 – 75.00.

Neutral gray antique convertible, with planter, backlighted,
8½" long, 5½" high, signed "BUCKINGHAM CERAMICS,"
$55.00 – 65.00.

Two-piece Art Deco green coach, elaborately molded with
three amber windows, marked "J-316," rests on a bronzed
wire base, 14½" long, 10¼" high, $85.00 – 100.00.

Cream outlined in gold "Lover's Lane" planter and
TV light, two bicycle riders superimposed against a
picket fence, 9½" wide, 6" high, $100.00 – 120.00.

HOME FOR CHRISTMAS IN THE 1950s

Christmas Memories of the 1950s

Courtesy of the National Christmas Center
3427 Lincoln Highway, Paradise, PA 17562

A sign in front of the exhibit reads as follows:

In those days we liked Ike (Eisenhower) and we loved Lucy. Father knew best but Uncle Miltie made us laugh. Bing Crosby was dreaming of a White Christmas while Rudolph and Frosty became part of our family celebration. Greeting cards were fondly displayed and our stockings were hung by the chimney with care.

Our local Five & Dime was stocked full with our favorite tree trimmings, including those new plastic ornaments, silvery tinsel, and fascinating bubble lights. What we put under the tree was just as important as what we put on it. Lionel trains traveled a constant circle and the Nativity set reminded us what it was all about. On Christmas morning we'd awake to delight in finding the treasure trove left for us by Santa and anxiously looked forward to our grand family gathering for dinner.

Shown is a portion of a room in the National Christmas Center permitting visitors to enjoy a nostalgic trip back to the 1950s.

A young boy wearing his new cowboy outfit and holding a prized teddy bear. Note the white horse TV lamp on the television.

The same boy in the same room, but the room now has a decorated tree and a dog TV lamp on the television set.

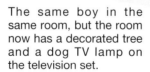

A chartreuse TV lamp on the same TV set shown in the preceding picture.

A fawn TV lamp with pressed glass flowers on a TV set with a round picture screen.

Typical TVs of the 1950s and 1960s included both tabletop and console models. Television lamps were attractively displayed on both types.

Television was demonstrated around 1926 and used in the 1930s experimentally. World War II affected TV development, and television became popular in the late 1940s. Color TV emerged in the mid-1950s, and sales of it eclipsed those for black and white television in the late 1960s.

Arvin, for example, in October 1950 offered a complete line of TVs ranging from $129.95 to $379.95. By the mid-1960s, prices for larger models ranged from $400.00 to $600.00. More elaborate console combinations sold from $700.00 to $2,000.00.

Popular brands of televisions included the following:

- Magnavox
- ITI Guest Television
- Hallicrafters
- Telefunken
- Westinghouse
- Sears Roebuck
- Montgomery Ward
- Sparton
- Stewart-Warner
- Sylvania
- Victor

- Olympic
- Admiral
- Andrea
- Arvin
- CBS-Columbia
- Coronado
- Crosley
- Deico
- Du Mont
- Emerson
- Fada

- General Electric
- Zenith
- Stromberg-Carlson
- Silvertone
- Sentinel
- RCA
- Raytheon/Belmont
- Pilot
- Motorola

WFIL

RADIO AND TELEVISION · 46TH AND MARKET STS. · TELEPHONE EVERGREEN 2-4700

PHILADELPHIA 39, PA.

April 3, 1961

NAME: _Jeanne Copeland_
ADDRESS: _1103 Agnew Dr. D.H._

This letter will serve as your admission to the video tape recording of "American Bandstand" at Willow Grove Park. This program will be taped on Saturday, April 15, 1961 to be aired at a later date.

The theme of this program will be the "Bandstand Fun House Party". We suggest you dress accordingly - slacks, sport clothes, etc.

Admission is by invitation only, and you must be prepared to show identification at the door. This letter is not transferable.

Willow Grove Park will be opened especially for our "Bandstand Fun House Party". Please be at the park Saturday Morning, April 15 at 10:30 A. M. and enter by the main gate at Easton and Welsh Roads.

The attached release form must be signed by your parent or guardian and turned in before you enter the park.

Sincerely yours,

Joe Novenson, Producer
"American Bandstand"

RADIO AND TELEVISION DIVISION TRIANGLE PUBLICATIONS, INC.

WFIL-AM · FM · TV, Philadelphia, Pa./ WNBF-AM · FM · TV, Binghamton, N.Y./ WLYH-TV, Lebanon, Pa.
WFBG-AM · TV, Altoona, Pa./ WNHC-AM · FM · TV, New Haven, Conn./ KFRE-AM · TV · KRFM, Fresno, Cal.

Intending to be legally bound, I hereby give WFIL-TV (radio and television, Triangle Publications, Inc.), ABC-TV, (American Broadcasting-Paramount Theatres, Inc.), Click Corporation and Dick Clark and their respective successors and assigns, the right to copyright, use and publish for any lawful purpose whatsoever, including advertising, trade pictorial art, the photographs taken, including all reproductions thereof, whether used in connection with his/her own or a fictitious name, and whether he/she appear in said reproductions in whole or in part, and I agree that this may be done without first submitting to me proofs for approval; and I further agree to release WFIL-TV, ABC, Click, Dick Clark and any sponsor of the program and it's advertising agents from any and all claims for loss or damage to persons or property.

DATE _April 14th 1961_

SON OR DAUGHTER'S NAME _Jeanne Copeland_

PARENT'S SIGNATURE _Mrs Robert Copeland_

Suggestions on getting to Willow Grove Park:

The 9:05 A. M. Reading Railroad Train from 12th and Market to Willow Grove Park or the Broad Street Subway to Broad and Olney, then number 55 Bus to Willow Grove which runs every twelve minutes.

LEH & CO., Allentown, PA – Christmas Catalog 1959.

Lovely Lamps highlight your home . . . .

22-45

22-43

22-16

22-2

22-13

22-3

22-49

22-7

22-14

22-2 Wrought Iron Pin-Up Lamp. Stunning jet black mesh wire base, black arm. 6" white and gold parchment shade. Overall height 10½". . . . . 1 book

22-3 Schrader Pin-Up Lamp. Polished brass planter lamp with 8" linen on parchmentized paper. 10" overall height, choice of red or green shade. . . . . 1 book

22-4 Modern Metal Adjustable Shade and Base Pin-Up Lamp. Smart design. Extends from wall 8 inches. Choice of black, pink, or green. . . . . 1 book

22-6 Hall China Table Lamp. Hand painted leaf design on concave china column mounted on brass base. Rayon shade. 3-way lighting. Overall height 28". . . . . 3½ books

22-7 Phil-Mar Figurine Lamp. Handsome "Mare and Foal" ebony ceramic base. Overall height 25" with a beautiful 16" red fiberglas shade. . . . . 2⅜ books

22-8 Plasto Modern Lamp. Distinctive modern design. Fiberglas drum shade. Palestic base. White and black combination. Overall height 31½". . . . . 2½ books

22-10 Colonial Lamp. Authentic reproduction. Highly polished base and shade holder. Glass shade in milk white with gold star design. 11" high. . . . . 1½ books

22-12 Universal Vanity and Bed Lamp Set. 3 pcs. Polished brass and star trimmed milk white glass. Two 9½" vanities and one 9½" bed lamp. . . . . 2½ books

22-13 Milk White Hobnail Lamp. Highly polished brass trim, clear crystal chimney. Height 17". 3-way socket with key switch. 7" shade. . . . . 2½ books

Choose your gifts from this great Catalog. Here you'll find the finest selection of famous name merchandise you could possibly wish for. Names you know, merchandise you need, quality that's of the highest.

Page 26

Top Value Stamps Redemption Store Catalog.

15 Pole Room Divider. Four adjustable black shelves, each 10" x 35". Pair brass poles, adjustable 7' x 9' to 8' x 11". (802-470) 7-2/5 Books

Pole Room Divider Add-On Unit, includes 1 brass pole and 4 black shelves, for use with basic unit above. (Not shown) Available at larger Gift Centers or special order only. (802-466) 6 Books

16 "Four Seasons" Plaques. Gold finished metal with wood frames and brass hangers. 6" x 20" (802-371) Set of Four. 4-1/5 Books

17 Classic Swans gracefully molded into 3 pc. Planter Set. Planting area in 3 pieces of varying heights. 11", 6", 5". (404-327) 2 Books

18 Matador Figure. Expertly sculptured ceramic. Wood grain finish. Hand decorated. 10 ½" high. (405-167) 1-3/5 Books

19 Charging Bull. Ceramic in wood stain finish. Sharply detailed. 6½" high, 14" long. (404-159) 2 Books

20 RED WING Console set. 10" Bowl with matching 4¼" candleholders. White (401-830) 1 Book*

21 win Swan Vase or Planter with bone white velvet mat glaze. 11" high. (403-733) 1 Book*

22 Pair Houdon Busts reproduced from the originals by famous French sculptor. Ivory antique finish. 9" high. (403-501) 2 Books

23 3 Piece Console Set. Use as three planters. Persimmon. (403-725) 1 Book*

24 Table Lamp, ceramic base finished in a textured glaze. Walnut shaft. 14" shade of nubby fabric. Three way switch. 31½" high. (803-502) 3-1/5 Books

25 Swan Planter Lamp. Ceramic swan, hand decorated. 12" high. (803-338) 1-2/5 Books*

26 Floor Tree Lamp. 61" tall, 3-light. Gold color enamel. Adjustable shades 4¾" diameter. (803-452) 5 Books

27 Masterpiece Miniatures. Color prints framed in brass. 6" diam. Set of 4. (402-727) 4/5 Book

28 Pair of Provincial Polished Brass Candelabras with 6 white taper candles. 9" high, 8" wide. (404-525) 1 Book

29 Window Planter, brass finish hangers with six ceramic jardiniers in matte white finish. Fits any double window 18" wide by 21" high or larger. (803-841) 2 Books

30 Pair Clover Cluster Shelves for your knick-knacks, plants or figurines. 13½" x13½" overall, 5 x 9" shelf. Brass finish. (403-295) 1-2/5 Books

*Flowers, plants, and candles not included.

PAGE 87

1961 Gold Bond gift book catalog.

1956 SEARS, ROEBUCK AND CO. FALL AND WINTER CATALOG - PGS. 820, 824

824 .. SEARS, ROEBUCK AND CO. 3F

Harmony House TV and Novelty Lamps

M Here's the perfect pot for your TV .. a sleek black panther in gleaming glazed pottery. Emits a soft indirect, glare-free light. Socket for bulb in back. 19 in. long. Mailable. Shipping weight 5 lbs.
21 H U2007....... $3.69

N Graceful black metal gazelle on gleaming brass plated steel base. Black mesh metal reflector, Fiberglas lined to diffuse soft light. 11¾-in. high overall. Takes 25-watt bulb, not incl. Mailable. Shpg. wt. 4 lbs.
21 H U2917...... $4.89

P Pottery Planter TV L 4¼-in. deep plant removable. 7½x4x9½ overall. No plants. color black metal 1 black planter or b plated base. H H l Chartreuse planter. S wt. 4 lbs.
21 H U2918. ...... $4

1957 SEARS, ROEBUCK AND CO. FALL AND WINTER CATALOG - PGS. 820, 824

Pottery Planter Lamp. A style that's increasing in popularity. Multiple-glazed black and white pottery base with jet black panther. 18x8-in. shade of gold-color decorated white fiber glass. Plants not included. Just picture a pair in your own home.
21 D T7530—About 22½ in. high. Wt. 11 lbs.. .Each $9.37

820 SEARS P

Decorative Accessory Lamps

BB New! Picture Lite. Illuminated picture of Sallman's "Head of Christ." Small bulb at side (included). Antiqued ivory finish wood frame, metal shadow box. 9½ in. high, 7½ in. wide.
21 D 2042—Shipping weight 4 lbs......... Each $5.74

CC New! Panther Planter Lamp. Highly glazed black finish pottery, flowing white accents. 1-way socket in back. Place for live plants.
21 D 2041—10½x5x14 in. long. Wt.7 lbs. 4 oz.. $5.74

DD New! Accent Lamp. Glazed pottery horse head. Soft light from 1-way socket in back. 7x16 in. long. State color med. brown or black.
21 D 2379—Shipping weight 7 lbs......... Each $6.44

EE Black Panther Lamp. Soft, glare-free illumination. Gleaming glazed pottery, 19 in. long. Realistic in appearance. Decorative conversation piece. 1-way socket for bulb in back.
21 D 2007—Shipping weight 5 lbs........ Each $3.74

1956/1957 Sears, Roebuck and Co. Fall and Winter Catalog.

PHIL-MAR COLORSCOPE

Shown in the next four pages is a fabulous find — an original salesman's sample box showing 60 sample colors available to stores wishing to carry TV lamps. The black simulated leather case with molded black plastic handle and two chrome clasps measures 18" wide x 13" high x 4" deep.

Each solid-shaped piece is numbered, measures 3¼" high, and has a felt bottom, and each number corresponds to the color on the chart. The pieces rest in cut-out sponge slots that protect them in transit. The collection consists of two layers, each showing 30 pieces.

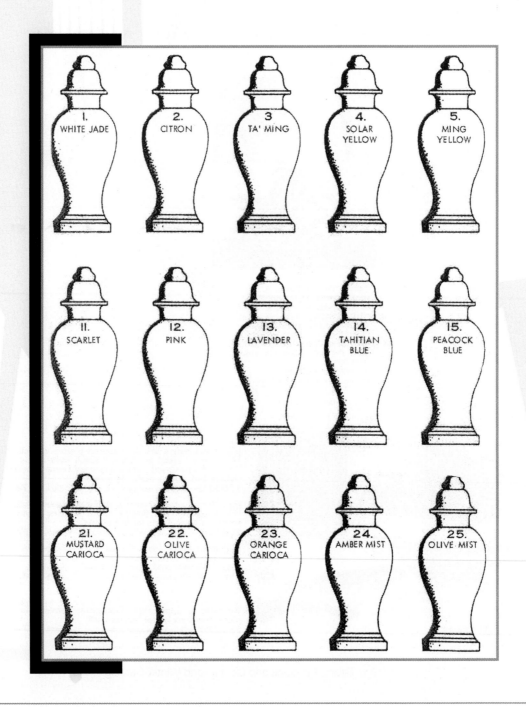

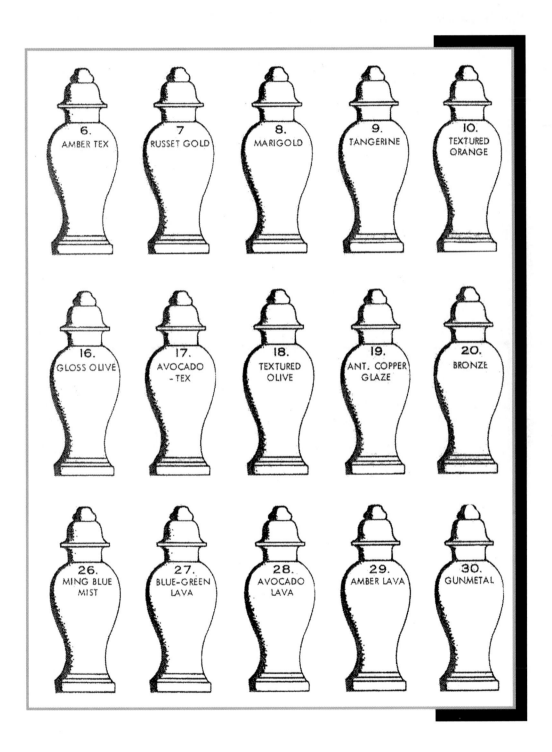

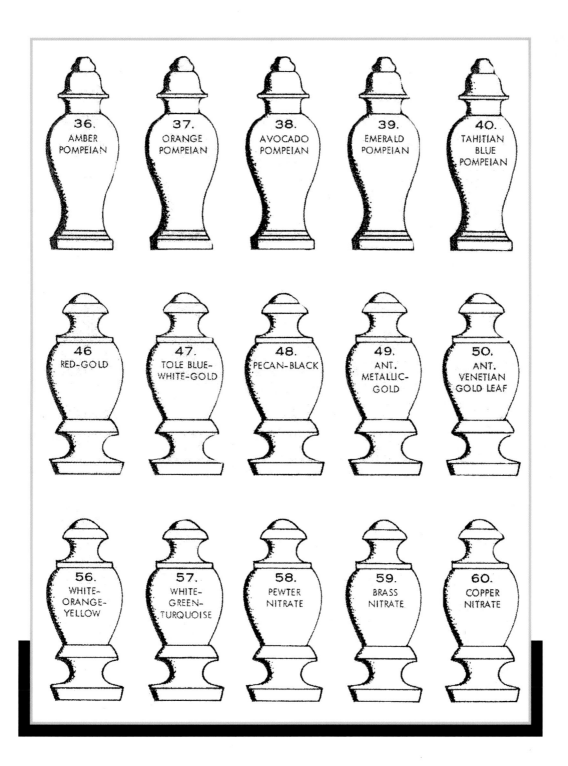

Airbrush — An atomizer with a variety of nozzles used to apply a fine spray of colored paint by means of compressed air.

Applied Decoration — Also called sprig; a molded piece of clay that has been hand-applied to greenware with slip. This is found occasionally on TV lamps.

Art Deco — Stylized forms and geometric designs; refers to decorative and architectural styling on objects from the 1920s and 1930s.

Backlighting — Refers to the light shining from the back of the lamp.

Blank — A ware that has not yet been decorated.

Bright Gold — Applied liquid gold paint decoration that comes out bright after being fired and requires no burnishing.

Cast — A TV lamp created from a wood, plaster, or metal mold. TV lamps were made of iron, chalkware, "chinaware," and other substances.

Casting — The process in which slip is poured into plaster molds and allowed to dry. Later the ware can be handled.

Ceramic — Any of various hard, brittle, heat-resistant, and corrosion-resistant materials made by firing clay and other minerals and metals in combination with oxygen.

Chalkware — A substance used to imitate marble that also aids in hardening plaster of Paris. Some TV lamps were made from this limestone substance and then colored.

China — High-quality porcelain or ceramic.

Chip — A flaw left after the removal of a small piece or section.

Cold Paint — Oil paint applied over a glaze for decorative purposes after the final firing. It is susceptible to chipping and wear.

Crackle (Craquelle) — A decorative effect showing a network of crazing cracks.

Crazing — Minute cracks in the glaze as a result of uneven contraction between the glaze and the body.

Cut-out Eyes — Molded sections on animals' faces from which the light shines through. Sometimes open and sometimes covered with jewels or marbles.

Decorative — Providing a sense of ornamentation or decoration to an area in a room.

Decorator — A person who applies the required decorative highlights.

Designer — A schooled or self-taught person responsible for conceiving, drawing, and executing a particular designed shape.

Detachable Figure — A figurine that can be removed and cleaned.

Eames, Charles (1907 – 1978) — A noted American designer. Often his name is used in relation to the TV lamp era.

Fiberglass — A material consisting of extremely fine glass fibers. Used in making various lamp parts; also called spun glass.

Figural — An ornamental figure usually cast in the form of a dog, cat, boat, leaf, shell, etc.

Fine China — A translucent china made of quality clays that when fired at high temperatures fuse into a hard, nonporous body.

Firing — Heat treatment of ceramics to secure resistance and permanency.

Funky — Characterized by originality and modishness; unconventional.

Glaze — A mixture, predominantly of oxides, applied to the surface of ceramic ware to form a moisture-impervious and often lustrous or ornamental coating.

Greenware — A piece that is finished and taken from the mold. It must dry further before being handled to any great extent.

Hairline — A slender line in a lamp signifying that stress and damage has occurred.

Harp — A harp-shaped wire on some earlier lamps that holds the shade in place.

Identification — A process by which an individual recognizes and classifies lamps into groups by manufacturers.

Imperfections — Defects or flaws; blemishes.

Incised — Etched; also called engraved. Incised marks or cuts are often glazed and fired, and are reliable means of identification.

Internal Lighting — Light coming from an interior source, such as the center of a floral TV lamp.

Manufacturer — A person, group, or factory that created and marketed TV lamps.

Marble Eyes — Matching marbles used, for example, as cat's eyes.

Marked — Having a noticeable means of identification such as a sticker or an incised mark. Also referred to as signed.

Metal Base — Thin, pressed sheets of metal, usually having geometric designs and brass finishes, that have been bent and formed into a lamp base.

Mint — Fresh, unused, original condition. Seldom found.

Nicked — Having a cut, a shallow notch, or an indentation on an edge or surface.

Novelty — A figural made for a chain store.

Planter — A decorative container for real or artificial flowers. Often serves as part of the TV lamp.

Plaster of Paris — A group of gypsum cements that form a paste when mixed with water and hardens into a solid.

Porcelain — A hard, white, translucent ceramic made by firing a pure clay and glazing it with various colored fusible materials. Produces a bell-like tone when tapped gently.

Pottery — Earthenware shaped from moist clay and hardened by heat.

Premium — Given away as part of a promotion through stamps, coupons, by route salesmen, etc.

Rampant — An animal depicted as rearing on its hind legs. Used especially with panthers and other big cats.

Recessed Bulb — A light that is out of the way in a remote, secluded location.

Reproduction — A copy of a vintage lamp or one produced in a contemporary fashion and sold as old; not genuine, spurious.

Retouch — To change or alter something from its original condition; especially, to repaint.

Retro — Looking back or referring to a former time in history.

Stamped — Impressed with a mark, design, or seal. Usually the company name will be discovered if the seal is intact. Some logos were very colorful and artistic.

Stamping — The process of applying ink to a rubber or sponge stamp and using pressure to transfer the stamp's design to the felt on the bottom of a lamp.

Sticker — A gummed or adhesive label showing a company's logo.

Stressed — Showing signs of distress. Used for a lamp in poor condition, one misused or worn out.

Torpedo Bulb — A bulb shaped in the fingerlike form of a torpedo. Torpedo bulbs are often used with TV lamps since they fit nicely and provide less heat.

TV Lamp — A colorful figural electrical device, usually ceramic, placed on or near a television in an earlier era to create additional light and prevent eyestrain.

Unique — One of a kind. A unique TV lamp is a knockout, one unusual or exceptional.

Unmarked — Not having a mark or any means of identification.

Variety Store Item — A TV lamp made for a variety of five-and-dime stores.

Vintage — Designates a year or period of origin, such as a 1950s TV lamp.

Vitrified — Nonporous, glass-like.

Ware — Pottery in any stage of manufacture (greenware, bisque ware, decorated ware).

Working Order — Functionality. A TV lamp in working order is one that functions and operates properly electrically.

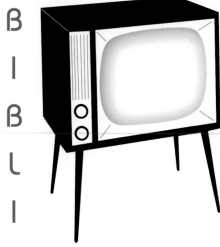

Devlin, Ron. "Kmart Began with Monroe Man's Vision." *The Morning Call,* January 23, 2002.

Duke, Harvey, *Pottery and Porcelain,* 8th Ed. New York: House of Collectibles, 1995.

Huxford, Sharon and Bob, eds. *Garage Sale & Flea Market Annual, 9th Ed.* Paducah, Kentucky: Collector Books, 2001.

Haeger: The Early and the Extraordinary. Wisconsin Pottery Association, 1998. tvlamps.net

Haeger Pottery Catalogs.

Haeger Potteries: Our History: 1871 – 1999.

Hollywood Ceramics. "Hollywood Ceramics Pixies."

Author interviews with Lynda Dawson and Bob and Peg Parks.

Maddux History. tvlamps.net

Kirshon, John W., ed. *Chronicle of America*. Mount Kisco, New York: 1989.

Morgan, Barbara J., ed. "America A to Z." *Reader's Digest.* Pleasantville, New York, 1997.

On This Day. Crescent Books, 1992.

Panati, Charles. *Panati's Extraordinary Origins of Everyday Things.* New York: Harper & Row, 1987.

———. *Panati's Parade of Fads, Follies, and Manias.* New York: Harper Perennial, 1991.

Payton, Leland and Crystal. *Turned On.* New York: Abbeyville Press, 1989.

Rinker, Harry L., ed. *Warman's 6th Edition Americana & Collectibles.* Radnor, Pennsylvania: 1993.

——— . *Warman's 7th Edition Americana & Collectibles.* Radnor, Pennsylvania: 1995.

Santiso, Tom. TV Lamps. Paducah, Kentucky: Collector Books, 1999.

———. "TV Lamps Shine for This Collector." *Antiques & Auction News,* February 11, 2000.

Schneider, Mike. *The Complete Cookie Jar Book.* Atglen, Pennsylvania: Schiffer Publishing Ltd., 2001.

Shepherd, Calvin. *'50s TV Lamps.* Atglen, Pennsylvania: Schiffer Publishing Ltd., 1998.

Wallechinsky, David and Amy Wallace. *The Book of Lists.* New York: Little, Brown and Company, 1993.

World Book Encyclopedia, The. Vol. 18. Chicago, Illinois: Field Enterprises, Inc., 1950.

GLASSWARE & POTTERY

6321	Carnival Glass, The Best of the Best, Edwards/Carwile	$29.95
6326	Collectible Cups & Saucers, Book III, Harran	$24.95
6344	Collectible Vernon Kilns, 2nd Edition, Nelson	$29.95
6331	Collecting Head Vases, Barron	$24.95
6830	Collector's Encyclopedia of Depression Glass, 17th Ed., Florence	$19.95
6629	Collector's Encyclopedia of Fiesta, 10th Ed., Huxford	$24.95
6609	Collector's Encyclopedia of Limoges Porcelain, 3rd Ed., Gaston	$29.95
5677	Collector's Encyclopedia of Niloak, 2nd Edition, Gifford	$29.95
5842	Collector's Encyclopedia of Roseville Pottery, Vol. 2, Huxford/Nickel	$24.95
6646	Collector's Ency. of Stangl Artware, Lamps, and Birds, 2nd Ed., Runge	$29.95
5680	Collector's Guide to Feather Edge Ware, McAllister	$19.95
6559	Elegant Glassware of the Depression Era, 11th Edition, Florence	$24.95
6126	Fenton Art Glass, 1907 – 1939, 2nd Edition, Whitmyer	$29.95
6320	Gaston's Blue Willow, 3rd Edition	$19.95
6127	The Glass Candlestick Book, Vol. 1, Akro Agate to Fenton, Felt/Stoer	$24.95
6648	Glass Toothpick Holders, 2nd Edition, Bredehoft	$29.95
6329	Glass Tumblers, 1860s to 1920s, Bredehoft/Sanford	$29.95
6562	The Hazel-Atlas Glass Identification and Value Guide, Florence	$24.95
5840	Heisey Glass, 1896 – 1957, Bredehoft	$24.95
5913	McCoy Pottery, Volume III, Hanson/Nissen	$24.95
6135	North Carolina Art Pottery, 1900 – 1960, James/Leftwich	$24.95
6335	Pictorial Guide to Pottery & Porcelain Marks, Lage	$29.95
5691	Post86 Fiesta, Identification & Value Guide, Racheter	$19.95
6037	Rookwood Pottery, Nicholson/Thomas	$24.95
6925	Standard Encyclopedia of Carnival Glass, 10th Ed., Edwards/Carwile	$29.95
6476	Westmoreland Glass, The Popular Years, 1940 – 1985, Kovar	$29.95
5924	Zanesville Stoneware Company, Rans/Ralston/Russell	$24.95

DOLLS & FIGURES

6315	American Character Dolls, Izen	$24.95
6317	Arranbee Dolls, The Dolls That Sell on Sight, DeMillar/Brevik	$24.95
6319	Barbie Doll Fashion, Volume III, 1975 – 1979, Eames	$29.95
6221	Barbie, The First 30 Years, 2nd Edition, Deutsch	$24.95
6134	Ency. of Bisque Nancy Ann Storybook Dolls, 1936 – 1947, Pardee/Robertson	$29.95
6451	Collector's Ency. of American Composition Dolls, Vol. II, Mertz	$29.95
6546	Collector's Ency. of Barbie Doll Exclusives, 3rd Ed., Augustyniak	$29.95
6636	Collector's Ency. of Madame Alexander Dolls, 1948 – 1965, Crowsey	$24.95
5904	Collector's Guide to Celebrity Dolls, Spurgeon	$24.95
5599	Collector's Guide to Dolls of the 1960s and 1970s, Sabulis	$24.95
6456	Collector's Guide to Dolls of the 1960s and 1970s, Vol. II, Sabulis	$24.95
6452	Contemporary American Doll Artists & Their Dolls, Witt	$29.95
6455	Doll Values, Antique to Modern, 8th Ed., DeFeo/Stover	$14.95
6937	Madame Alexander Collector's Dolls Price Guide #31, Crowsey	$14.95
5611	Madame Alexander Store Exclusives & Limited Editions, Crowsey	$24.95
5689	Nippon Dolls & Playthings, Van Patten/Lau	$29.95
6929	Official Precious Moments Collector's Guide to Figurines, 2nd Ed., Bomm	$16.95
5253	Story of Barbie, 2nd Ed., Westenhouser	$24.95
6642	20th Century Paper Dolls, Young	$19.95
4880	World of Raggedy Ann Collectibles, Avery	$24.95

JEWELRY & ACCESSORIES

6122	Brilliant Rhinestones, Aikins	$24.95
6323	Christmas Pins, Past & Present, 2nd Edition, Gallina	$19.95
4850	Collectible Costume Jewelry, Simonds	$24.95
5675	Collectible Silver Jewelry, Rezazadeh	$24.95
6453	Collecting Costume Jewelry 101, Carroll	$24.95
6468	Collector's Ency. of Pendant & Pocket Watches, 1500 – 1950, Bell	$24.95
4940	Costume Jewelry, A Practical Handbook & Value Guide, Rezazadeh	$24.95
5812	Fifty Years of Collectible Fashion Jewelry, 1925 – 1975, Baker	$24.95
6330	Handkerchiefs: A Collector's Guide, Guarnaccia/Guggenheim	$24.95
6464	Inside the Jewelry Box, Pitman	$24.95
5695	Ladies' Vintage Accessories, Bruton	$24.95
1181	100 Years of Collectible Jewelry, 1850 – 1950, Baker	$9.95
6645	100 Years of Purses, Aikins	$24.95
6232	Plastic Jewelry of the 20th Century, Baker	$24.95
6337	Purse Masterpieces, Schwartz	$29.95
6039	Signed Beauties of Costume Jewelry, Brown	$24.95
4850	Unsigned Beauties of Costume Jewelry, Brown	$24.95
5923	Vintage Jewelry for Investment & Casual Wear, Edeen	$24.95

FURNITURE

3716	American Oak Furniture, Book II, McNerney	$12.95
1118	Antique Oak Furniture, Hill	$7.95
6474	Collector's Guide to Wallace Nutting Furniture, Ivankovich	$19.95
3906	Heywood-Wakefield Modern Furniture, Rouland	$18.95
6338	Roycroft Furniture & Collectibles, Koon	$24.95
6343	Stickley Brothers Furniture, Koon	$24.95
1885	Victorian Furniture, Our American Heritage, McNerney	$9.95

ARTIFACTS, GUNS, KNIVES, TOOLS, PRIMITIVES

1868	Antique Tools, Our American Heritage, McNerney	$9.95
1426	Arrowheads & Projectile Points, Hothem	$7.95
6021	Arrowheads of the Central Great Plains, Fox	$19.95
5685	Indian Artifacts of the Midwest, Book IV, Hothem	$19.95
6130	Indian Trade Relics, Hothem	$29.95
6565	Modern Guns, Identification & Values, 15th Ed., Quertermous	$16.95
6567	Paleo-Indian Artifacts, Hothem	$29.95
2164	Primitives, Our American Heritage, McNerney	$9.95
6031	Standard Knife Collector's Guide, 4th Ed., Ritchie & Stewart	$14.95

PAPER COLLECTIBLES & BOOKS

5902	Boys' & Girls' Book Series, Jones	$19.95
6623	Collecting American Paintings, James	$29.95
6553	Collector's Guide to Cookbooks, Daniels	$24.95
1441	Collector's Guide to Post Cards, Wood	$9.95
6627	Early 20th Century Hand-Painted Photography, Ivankovich	$24.95
6936	Leather Bound Books, Boutiette	$24.95
6234	Old Magazines, Clear	$19.95
3973	Sheet Music Reference & Price Guide, 2nd Ed., Guiheen/Pafik	$19.95

TOYS & MARBLES

2333	Antique & Collectible Marbles, 3rd Ed., Grist	$9.95
6649	Big Book of Toy Airplanes, Miller	$24.95
4945	G-Men and FBI Toys, Whitworth	$18.95
6633	Hot Wheels, The Ultimate Redline Guide, 2nd Ed., Clark/Wicker	$29.95
6466	Matchbox Toys, 4th Ed., 1947 to 2003, Johnson	$24.95
6638	The Other Matchbox Toys, 1947 to 2004, Johnson	$19.95
6840	Schroeder's Collectible Toys, Antique to Modern Price Guide, 10th Ed	$17.95
6650	Toy Car Collector's Guide, 2nd Ed., Johnson	$24.95

OTHER COLLECTIBLES

5814	Antique Brass & Copper Collectibles, Gaston	$24.95
1880	Antique Iron, McNerney	$9.95
6447	Antique Quilts & Textiles, Aug/Roy	$24.95
1128	Bottle Pricing Guide, 3rd Ed., Cleveland	$7.95
6345	Business & Tax Guide for Antiques & Collectibles, Kelly	$14.95
3718	Collectible Aluminum, Grist	$16.95
6342	Collectible Soda Pop Memorabilia, Summers	$24.95
5676	Collectible Souvenir Spoons, Book II, Bednersh	$29.95
6625	Collector's Encyclopedia of Bookends, Kuritzky/DeCosta	$29.95
5666	Collector's Encyclopedia of Granite Ware, Book II, Greguire	$29.95
5906	Collector's Guide to Creek Chub Lures & Collectibles, 2nd Ed., Smith	$29.95
6558	The Ency. of Early American Sewing Machines, 2nd Ed., Bays	$29.95
5683	Fishing Lure Collectibles, Vol. 1, Murphy/Edmisten	$29.95
6931	Fishing Lure Collectibles, The Modern Era, Murphy	$29.95
6932	Flea Market Trader, 15th Ed.	$12.95
6458	Fountain Pens, Past & Present, 2nd Edition, Erano	$24.95
6933	Garage Sale & Flea Market Annual, 14th Edition	$19.95
2216	Kitchen Antiques, 1790 – 1940, McNerney	$14.95
5603	19th Century Fishing Lures, Carter	$29.95
6322	Pictorial Guide to Christmas Ornaments & Collectibles, Johnson	$29.95
5835	Racing Collectibles, Editors of Racing Collector's Magazine	$19.95
3443	Salt & Pepper Shakers IV, Guarnaccia	$18.95
6570	Schroeder's Antiques Price Guide, 23rd Edition 2005	$14.95
5007	Silverplated Flatware, Revised 4th Edition, Hagan	$18.95
6647	Star Wars Super Collector's Wish Book, 3rd Ed., Carlton	$29.95
6632	Value Guide to Gas Station Memorabilia, 2nd Ed., Summers/Priddy	$29.95
5925	The Vintage Era of Golf Club Collectibles, John	$29.95
6036	Vintage Quilts, Aug/Newman/Roy	$24.95
4935	The W.F. Cody Buffalo Bill Collector's Guide with Values, Wojtowicz	$24.95

This is only a partial listing of the books on antiques that are available from Collector Books. All books are well illustrated and contain current values. Most of these books are available from your local bookseller, antique dealer, or public library. If you are unable to locate certain titles in your area, you may order by mail from COLLECTOR BOOKS, P.O. Box 3009, Paducah, KY 42002-3009. Customers with Visa, MasterCard, or Discover may phone in orders from 7:00 a.m. to 5:00 p.m. CT, Monday – Friday, toll free 1-800-626-5420, or online at www.collectorbooks.com. Add $4.00 for postage for the first book ordered and 50¢ for each additional book. Include item number, title, and price when ordering. Allow 14 to 21 days for delivery.